1, 2, 3, 4,
6, 7, 8, 9, 10, 11
13, 14, 15, 16, 17, 18
20 (21) (22 T) (23 T) (24 T)   25 - 27 N?.
M   T   W   Th   F

28?, 29, 30, 31,
___

J·1 FIRS-

Medicine, Morals and the Law

SHEILA McLEAN
*Department of Forensic
Medicine and Science*
and
GERRY MAHER
*Department of Jurisprudence,
University of Glasgow*

Gower   1983

Published by
Gower Publishing Company Limited,
Gower House, Croft Road, Aldershot, Hampshire GU11 3HR,
England

British Library Cataloguing in Publication Data

McLean, Sheila
    Medicine, morals and the law.
    1. Medical ethic
    I. Title   II. Maher, Gerry
    174'2   R724

    ISBN 0-566-00533-6

Printed and bound in Great Britain by
Robert Hartnoll Limited,   e.141.1 25/6
Bodmin, Cornwall.

Contents

Preface

In recent years, medicine and the medical professions have become the focus of public attention and controversy. Doubtless the reason behind the development of some of this interest and discussion can be found in the topicality and news-worthiness of the issues concerned, features particularly noticeable in the thalidomide controversy and the continuing public interest in the development of new techniques, such as in the heart transplant programmes being carried out in a limited number of hospitals. There are, however, deeper reasons for a re-appraisal of medical practice which make it appropriate to explore and explain some of the overlapping concerns of the disciplines of medicine, morals and the law.

One such reason is the phenomenal change in medical practice due to recent developments in medical research and technology, and the clinical application of innovations in other disciplines. This is particularly true in relation to developments in drugs and machines, developments which have provoked a multitude of problems for the medical profession and which can no longer be seen as entirely medical or narrowly technical in nature. As doctors, and indeed others involved in medicine, are confronted by an almost overwhelming proliferation of 'cures' and 'lifesavers' in the form of pharmaceutical and technological innovations, equally they are more and more confronted with decisions which relate as much to dying and death as they do to the more traditional decisions about type of therapy or cure, all of which raise perplexing ethical and legal problems. When, if at all, does the switching-off of life support machines amount to murder and what is the legal or moral status of decisions not to treat handicapped babies? Are modern methods of inducing abortion moral or indeed legal? Who should be the first patient to try out a new drug of potential benefits to himself or to others, and who takes such decisions?

The existence of these and many more questions points to the second reason for the assessment of medical perspectives in the light of law and morals, namely that the very role of medicine and its practitioners has been the focus of considerable re-appraisal. The recent Reith Lectures sought to expose and 'unmask' modern medicine[1] and Illich begins his influential critique of the medical profession by writing: 'The medical establishment has become a major threat to health'.[2] This controversy involves a fundamental questioning of the place of medicine in society and challenges the view that medicine is an autonomous descipline, isolated from other perspectives, a purely technical affair best and most safely left to the experts, that is to those trained in medicine.

It is also true, of course, that doctors themselves have become more aware lately of the social and indeed political role of medicine, and The Lancet and the British Medical Journal regularly carry items not only on medical ethics and law relating to doctors, but also on more general social and political problems such as unemployment, inflation, the legislative process and the distribution of finance and resources in health care.

It should not be too difficult to understand why it is to the fields of morals and the law that doctors have turned in seeking solutions to these problems, for morals and the law share one important characteristic. Both provide means of evaluating and guiding human action, and both are practical in that they give the means to obtain the answers (if not the answers themselves) to the question of what to do in a given situation.

Thus, morals provides us with ways of characterising actions as good or bad, just or unjust. (Morals is sometimes used to refer to the views in fact held by people on certain matters, as opposed to ethics or critical morality which refers to the reasons, and the structure of reasons, for such beliefs. Here, however, we are using morals more in this latter sense, that is as a critical mode of enquiry into matters of value). Such lofty matters were for long left in medical practice to the field of 'medical ethics' which itself became an autonomous medical-based specialism, and of relevance to the practitioner only in rare and unusual cases. However, recent developments have shown that medical ethics cannot be an isolated discipline, and that questions of values permeate the whole field of medical practice. It is also worth noting a trend in recent moral theory towards adopting a more practically based approach by attempting to apply general ethical theories to concrete moral problems, and in pursuit of this goal philosophers have devoted some considerable energy to the discussion of medical-oriented problems.

But if the role of morals is to provide a means of assessing and guiding our actions, why should the law be consulted by medical practitioners in addition to morals? One reason for this is the obvious one that very often law and morals do not coincide in the guidance they offer. Indeed, it is an important issue in the present context to what extent the law should enforce moral judgements, an issue on which heated debate has raged in areas such as abortion and euthanasia. Again, all of us may be caught in practical situations where moral belief and legal rule conflict. That there can be discrepancies between law and morals is itself a feature of another important point about law, namely that on the whole it provides guidance by means of hard-and-fast and relatively clear-cut rules. The very existence of such rules which can be enforced in both criminal and civil law, ensures that doctors cannot ignore the law whatever its content.

In this book, a number of topics have been selected as highlighting the current debates in medical practice. Although in one sense the perspective is medical, in that these are problems which are actually faced by medical practitioners, it is a necessary part of the general argument of the book that such problems are not to be seen as purely 'medical'. The differing points of view of law and morals, though not necessarily the only or even the most important perspectives, are nonetheless valuable ways of reflecting upon such matters. It would also be a fundamental error to regard law and morals as matters for discussion only by 'experts' and it is hoped that doctors and many others will find this book a useful contribution to the discussion engendered by medical practice.

We have attempted to provide a general introduction to some of the most topical issues facing medicine, from the perspectives of morals and the law. The discussion is aimed at the general reader, and therefore, of necessity, many deep and contentious arguments from law or philosophy, have been dealt with rather more briefly and superficially than might satisfy an expert in these fields. It is hoped, however, that this book will provide at least a starting point to a wider consideration of these issues, and reflect some of the debates which continue to surround the practice of contemporary medicine.

In preparing this book, we owe many debts of gratitude, in particular to Tom Campbell, Professor of Jurisprudence, at the University of Glasgow, who read all the chapters carefully, and whose comments and criticisms were of immense value to us. Mrs. G. Robertson was unfailingly helpful and accurate in the typing of the manuscript, and Mrs. M. Harrison also gave freely of her time and assistance during its preparation. Richard Susskind devoted considerable time and effort to proof reading the final version, and we are most grateful to him. Finally, we must thank Professor W.A. Harland, Regius Professor of Forensic Medicine, Glasgow University, for his generosity with departmental time and facilities, without which this book could not have been completed.

NOTES

1.   Kennedy, I., The Unmasking of Medicine, London, George Allen and Unwin, 1981.
2.   Illich, I., Limits to Medicine. Medical Nemesis: The Expropriation of Health, Harmondsworth, Penguin Books, 1977 edition, at p. 11.

1 The Sanctity of Life

The obvious starting-place for any discussion of ethical and legal aspects of medical practice is to consider the doctrine of the sanctity of life. Certainly life is something protected in all legal systems, though we should note the variation, both historical and current, in the type and extent of this protection. Life is also often considered to be an important value, if not indeed the supreme value, in most contemporary systems of morality. Furthermore it is often said that the value of life permeates all medical practice and is the focal point of proper medical ethics. Thus the Geneva Convention Code of Medical Ethics (1949) includes the vow that:

> I will maintain the utmost respect for human life from the time of conception; even under threat. I will not use my medical knowledge contrary to the laws of humanity.

However despite the evident stress on the value of life, it is obvious that in fact we do not place as much value on life as we appear to, and that we certainly do not treat life as 'sacred' or absolute in the sense that life is treated as completely inviolable. Many societies which proffer a belief in the sanctity of life also accept capital punishment and war.

This gap between our easy acceptance of the supreme importance of life in theory and our willingness to compromise this value in practice is disadvantageous in two ways. One is that this inconsistency is no mere mistake or misapprehension of some factual situation, but is rather a device for making moral choices without openly considering the issues (this might be called the ideological function of the belief in the sanctity of life since it serves to divert our attention from difficult choices). Secondly, and following on from this point, many difficult but important moral issues are left undiscussed or inconsistently resolved. To raise explicitly the actual value which we are prepared to give to life opens up many issues in medical practice which need to be identified and tackled directly.

On deeper reflection it should not come as any great surprise to discover that what passes for the sanctity of life does not really mean taking life as an ultimate value in the sense that it overrides all other possible moral considerations. The nearest point which the Hippocratic Oath takes to this position is the less direct promise that 'the health of my patient will be my first consideration' (1947 version), but this does not, of course, mean that it is the only proper consideration. It is sometimes thought that the traditional doctrine of Christianity, whose historical influence is immense in this area and from where we derive the very idea of the 'sanctity' of life, supports the strong view of life as the absolute or supreme value. But, as we shall see, this doctrine does have one significant limitation, namely that it applies only to the lives of human beings. The nearest view that can be found to an absolute version of the sanctity of life is the idea of 'reverence for life' associated with the writings and works of Albert Schweitzer.

For instance, Schweitzer wrote[1]:

> I cannot but have reverence for all that is called life.
> I cannot avoid compassion for all that is called life.
> This is the beginning and foundation of morality.

And even more strongly[2]:

> Ethics thus consists in this, that I experience the necessity of practising the same reverence for life toward all will-to-live, as toward my own. Therein I have already the needed fundamental principle of morality. It is good to maintain and cherish life; it is evil to destroy and check life.

But as Singer has pointed out[3], Schweitzer's own career as a missionary and doctor in Africa shows that an ethic of reverence for all life cannot be maintained as an absolute practical principle.

For the work of any doctor presupposes at the least that the life of the patient is of greater value than the 'lives' of germs or parasites attacking the patient, and in Schweitzer's case the lives of the patients whom he cured were valued more highly than those of the animals or plants the patients would not have eaten if they had not been cured by him.

Further, there is little room in most systems of law and morals for an extreme form of pacifism whereby the taking of all life is wrong. This is so because in some situations, no matter what is done (or not done) life must be lost. The obvious illustration of this is the case of the morally appropriate response to an attack on one's own body. Thus for me to take no action against a murderous assailant is to arrange a priority of the value of lives whereby I must sacrifice my own life rather than ward off attack and risk killing my attacker. Of course, there are many fine gradations of moral significance in ways of killing and modes of responsibility for death, but if a sanctity of life doctrine is an absolute one it should embrace all such distinctions. It is the emphasis placed on responsibility for intentional actions by Christian-based ethics which explains why not all cases of causing death are condemned by the traditional doctrine of the sanctity of life. There is little support in most moral systems for absolute pacifism and many would think it to be a deficient moral code which forbade a right to self-defence (though the requirement of many legal systems that the force used must be reasonable in relation to the nature of the attack, even if in some circumstances this results in killing, adopts a sound moral view).

What we see then is that the broad idea of the sanctity of life is open to a variety of interpretations which need to be kept distinct and which the notion of 'sanctity' does not by itself make clear. It is one thing to say that life, simply as life, has some value but another to assert that life is the paramount factor in any set of moral considerations. Or take the idea of sanctity of life as meaning that it is always wrong to kill. Does this principle apply without exception, or may we take life when to do so results in other lives being saved? Again, if life is sacred, does it follow that it is always right to save life, and, if this is the case, is the duty to save life the highest moral duty? It is evident that the doctrine of sanctity of life can be applied to many different types of situation, and any discussion of the doctrine must make clear those various distinctions.

To whom does the doctrine apply?

One other significant feature about understanding sanctity of life is the range of application of the doctrine, or in other words, to whose lives does it apply?   It was seen that Schweitzer's principle of reverence for life was compromised in his own practice by the relative disvalue he placed on the 'lives' of germs and parasites which attacked the health of his patients.   Now, one possible objection to this reply is to ask in what sense it can be said that germs or parasites have 'life' or at least a life which has moral relevance.

Perhaps it is true that much common morality does see only humans as having life or only human life as being of moral value.   If there is such a belief, it is difficult to comprehend it as anything other than an unquestioned acceptance of a theological doctrine which on further reflection would be thought by many to be out of place in a modern system of ethics.   The traditional Christian doctrine of the sanctity of life extends only to human beings but the reason for this limitation is to be found in the idea of ensoulation, that is that only humans possess a soul.   But, it might be thought, the possession of a soul (especially an immortal one) hardly shows why human life must be taken as sacred and inviolable.   Indeed if anything the mortality of the flesh as contrasted with the immortality of the soul gives the former a significant disvalue in terms of the latter.   What is behind the prohibition of killing in Christian ethics is the idea that man cannot usurp God's prerogative in choosing the time of death.   But we should note that in itself this view provides us with no reason why it is not also wrong to destroy any other life forms.

Modern philosphers have shown that once we reject this theological-based doctrine, the moral status of life-forms other than human beings becomes less clear-cut and more problematic.   Indeed some writers have detected in many current moral beliefs the idea of speciesism, that is the view that the species homo sapiens is morally superior to other species without any morally relevant distinction between humans and others being adduced.   Certainly the argument that animals have 'rights', or rather moral status, has been put convincingly, and many of the ways in which humans at present use animals, e.g. killing them to use their fur for fashionable clothing, can be condemned outright as morally iniquitous, and not just because human beings like to observe wildlife or take satisfaction from its existence. Rather more difficult are cases where animals are killed in order to provide food for human beings. Many of the objections to this practice stem from the questionable modes of rearing and slaughtering animals, but there are also difficulties about the general correctness of killing animals for eating, when there are alternative forms of food (which may indeed be better for our health). But it would equally be a form of speciesism to assert, without more evidence or argument, that animals are morally superior to (say) vegetable life-forms. Again it is a point of fact that in our present world we do not produce sufficient food synthetically, and if nutrition is a necessary feature of continued living (as it seems to be), then ranking of priorities (of the lives of animals and vegetables) is an inescapable part of moral life. Now it clearly does not follow from this that it is impossible to make relevant distinctions between different types of life or existence (for example, by using the criterion of capacity to feel pain) but if a doctrine of sanctity of life is to be morally acceptable this argument has to be explicitly made rather than silently assumed.

In the context of the present general discussion many of these problems must be left unexplored, as our concern is with the practice of human medicine. However there is one part of the general moral debate on the status of animals which does impinge directly upon human medicine, that is the use of animals in medical experimentation.[4] It is historically the case that many of the drugs now commonly used in medical practice were developed or perfected by use of animal experimentation. This involves a variety of practices. One method often used is deliberately to infect a laboratory animal in order to gauge its reaction to doses of the drug being tested. Other methods include the giving of high doses of drugs to animals to measure reaction as an indication of the likely response by humans to treatment on a regime of the tested drugs.

These practices have more recently been called into question. There is indeed one view (associated mainly with the works of

Illich[5]) that very few drugs in modern medical use do improve health; on the contrary, it is argued, the overdependence and over-use of pharmaceutical products is a contributor to the increase in what are called iatrogenic or medically-induced illnesses. Even if we accept that some drugs are properly part of medical practice, questions remain as to their development and refinement. There are problems enough in the issue of medical experimentation on humans.[6] But it is simply an example of speciesism to assert boldly that it is permissible to conduct experiments on animals in order to provide safe, or safer, drugs for use in human medicine. Clearly if alternative methods of testing are available, then any consideration of the moral standing of animals should lead us to prefer the use of such alternatives. However, it could well be the case that the continued development of medical products does depend upon destroying the lives of animals for experimental purposes. Would this be morally permissible? Two extreme views give easy answers, but hardly leave us with satisfactory solutions. One is that of extreme pacifism or reverence for life which asserts that animal life simple as life must not be violated no matter what the consequences or potential consequences. Another extreme is the speciesist view that there is no real moral issue here at all. However it seems preferable to believe that there is a question of justification involved in our present practices of animal experimentation.

The use of animals in relation to human medicine has been discussed in some detail because it illustrates in a clear manner the major issues of moral theory in medical practice. Once we accept that there is a moral issue in the use of animals for experimentation, we can see a variety of ways of resolving the issue. Does animal life have value simply as life? If so, is this value of equal weight to the value of other life-forms, such as human life? If animal life has value can it ever be justifiably taken, or is all killing of animals for any purpose wrong? Although these important questions are not the direct concern of our present discussion, they do at least point to the sorts of issue that arise in considering the sanctity or value of human life, a topic to which we now turn.

The Boundaries of Human Life.

If we leave aside the question of the bearing of animal life for the doctrine of sanctity of life, we find that there are a number of problems even in restricting the discussion to the issue of the value of human life. One such concerns the boundaries of human life, or to put the matter another way, when can human life be said to begin and be said to end. Both of these issues have for long attracted the attention of theorists, but both have also been given direct practical relevance by modern technological based medical development. Thus, the traditional discussion of the moral standing of a human being before birth, a topic examined below in chapter 2, has taken on a new dimension by the development of in vitro fertilisation (so-called test-tube babies). Further, recent modes of maintaining the working of at least some bodily functions by the use of life-support machines have raised a number of difficulties about determining the stage of death, difficulties not just for moral theory but also for the law. Thus there are problems in answering such questions as whether a person in a state of permanent coma is alive or dead, or the moral and legal significance of switching off life-support machines.[7]

Some of these problems about the beginning and the end points of human life will be discussed in later chapters but it is worth stressing here that the importance of these matters is not purely that of seeking the proper definition of the phrase 'human life' but also that they bear upon more substantive moral issues. When we considered earlier the case of Schweitzer's preference for human life over the lives of germs and parasites, a possible objection was that it is a misleading use of the term 'life' to refer to the 'lives' of such entities. Similarly it might be thought that what is really at issue about abortion or terminating treatment is the proper definition of human life and that these matters can be decided solely on the basis of scientific or clinical criteria.

But to take these controversies simply as disputes about definitions, which could be solved by resort to biology textbooks, is a mistake. The reason why it would be a mistake to take such a view is that in the present context the terms 'life' or 'human life' are not neutral but are morally loaded, that is they are advanced as part of moral argument and not just to report scientific observation.

Often what people are prepared to count as 'human life' depends on what form of life they value and their reasons for doing so. Accordingly, some writers have argued that we would do better to concentrate our efforts on the substantive issues rather than get bogged down in seemingly semantic disputes as to whether germs, or animals, or foetuses, or the permanently comatose are truly alive or have life. This observation is of considerable value for it reminds us that the difficulty about the application of a value of life ethic is that much of what we actually do, and what we seek justification for, involves the taking or the disvaluing of life in some shape or form. It is simply an easy way out to argue that we do value life and then stipulate that life-forms which we do not respect are not really 'life'.

Why value human life?

It would be inconsistent with any satisfactory conception of proper ethical thinking simply to take human life, or life generally, as something of value without adducing reasons for this view. What is it about human life that we value? The central question in the theoretical debate on the 'sacredness' of life must surely be this one, and its centrality stems not only from the nature of theoretical arguments but also from its implications for practical action. Indeed if we had a clearer notion as to why and to what extent life is of value and what special considerations affect the value of human life, then we would be several steps nearer to a fuller understanding of several of the complex ethical issues of modern medical practice.

This is not to say that we cannot give reasons for placing value on human life; on the contrary, it is more likely that we will be faced with a number of arguments, many of them mutually inconsistent. Historically (as we noted earlier) the traditional reason given for the special value of human life is the possession of an immortal soul by all humans, and only by them. But we have noted that this belief in itself is not sufficient to support the doctrine of sanctity of life (in the sense of mortal life). More to the point, whatever the extent of religious belief today (and it should not be underestimated) religious doctrines can contribute to moral argument only by abandoning any special claim to unchallengeable and intrinsic correctness. In other words, we still need rational and logically consistent supporting arguments in order to provide acceptable moral standards in respect of the question of the value of human life. The two different approaches usually adopted (as with most moral issues) are those of utilitarianism on the one hand and respect for persons and autonomy-based ethics on the other. Not only are these two approaches to morality of relevance to the doctrine of sanctity of life and related issues, they can also be seen as contrasting perspectives on all moral issues in medical practice.

Utilitarianism is a label which has been applied to a variety of views and doctrines which share a common core of belief that assessment of moral good is to be made in relation to the amount of 'happiness' inherent in a state of affairs and that conduct is assessed as right or wrong depending upon its contribution to the total amount of such happiness. The crucial aspect about the morality of conduct is the examination of what consequences it has. For utilitarians, it is always right to increase happiness, and to achieve this we seek to maximise the good of pleasure and to minimise the evil of pain. The problems associated with this form of ethics are legion. Some are concerned with the conceptual adequacy of some of the key components of the theory, and the application of the standard of the greatest happiness of the greatest number as a practical mode of ethics. What, for instance, is the measurement of such happiness? The classical criteria of pleasure and pain have been abandoned in more modern versions of utilitarian theory but difficulties remain with proposed alternatives, such as the idea of preferences or interests. Further, apart from these problems of how to measure happiness there are also difficulties about the commensurability of happiness. Can one person's happiness be compared with another's happiness, or his lack of it? Another source of criticism of utilitarianism is that it presents a defective system of ethics. Thus with its concentration on consequentialist reasoning it has no place for the idea that some actions may be intrinsically right or wrong. Again, its emphasis on aggregating and maximising happiness appears to allow it to sanction on certain occasions the unfair treatment of minorities or individuals. This situation arises when the happiness of minorities is by-passed or ignored in order to increase the happiness of others by a greater amount.

However utilitarian-based theories have played a prominent role in arguments about the value of life, for they do seem to provide a plausible enough guide to many of the difficult cases. For although the criteria of pleasure and pain may be somewhat unrefined and difficult to apply in all situations, it still gives us a sure enough guide for many practical cases. Thus we can explain the essential wrongness of killing in terms of the pain and the deprivation of pleasure normally involved, an exception being where a person is living in pain and where killing would be justified if it would reduce the overall amount of pain. What is more, the capacity to experience pleasure and pain is not restricted to human beings. Accordingly utilitarians can show why it is wrong to kill or inflict injury on animals (and on the same basis may even provide arguments showing why the cases of killing of animals and vegetables differ, namely in the respective capacities to feel pain). Furthermore, the emphasis placed on the consequences of action offers further support for viewing killing as morally wrong. For if we did not condemn the taking of life or failed to uphold life as an important value, any notion of general social harmony and security would soon disappear.

Take also some of the more troublesome cases in medical practice, such as those concerning people in a state of permanent coma. Given that the permanently comatose do not experience pain and would not be aware of any threat to their continued existence, the switching off of a life-support machine may be justified. Indeed there might be great cost to society in maintaining life in such a case, e.g. by using a machine which might be used by someone else. Or take the case where we have detected gross abnormalities in a foetus, and we have to assess the propriety of abortion in such circumstances. The relevant calculation here will be about the chance of a happy life for such a child, whether its parents would be prepared to live with and support it, and so on. These questions may be difficult to answer in practice but they need not be rejected as impossible in principle.

However, although these examples may appear to reach acceptable conclusions, their underlying argument may also lead to more unacceptable outcomes when applied to other cases. One difficulty about utilitarian theories is that they provide no strong reasons why, once we have decided that someone's continued existence is unlikely to be 'happy', we should not proceed to kill that person. This reasoning may have a sort of plausibility in the case of the severely disabled or permanently comatose, but its range as a form of argument seems too wide. For example, I could adduce reasons for saying that persons of socio-economic class 4 or 5 or who belong to certain racial or religious minority groups, have not the remotest chance of enjoying a happy life or adding to the overall social happiness. And given certain assumptions about what constitutes a happy life, this conclusion might in one sense be true, for we do think that certain people have fewer 'chances' than others (say the children of a poor immigrant family as opposed to children of a well-off middle-class family). Such assessments are a common feature of the thinking of the sort of society in which we live. The only counter-consideration which utilitarianism can offer is to point to the threat to the general security of society if such reasoning were accepted, but any such consequences are merely contingent, and they may not exist in some situations, as where minorities are easily identifiable and can be distinguished from others. What is the weakest aspect of utilitarianism then, is that it gives no scope for consideration of the interests of an individual person as these appear to the particular person concerned.

Consider, for instance, the doctrine of 'actual and potential people', which has been advanced in utilitarian-based literature.[8] If the only morally significant aspect of a person is the individual's utility value (how much he or she contributes to the overall social well-being), then people are somehow 'replaceable'. On this basis it would be right to kill people with low utility now so that we can increase total utility by adding more people with higher utility. Utilitarianism may be able to accommodate some of the difficulties about comparing people with one another, but it is an unavoidable central part of the theory that no special interest is taken in persons merely because they are persons.

In contrast, the autonomy of the individual is at the forefront of the other broad approach to ethical theory which we identified earlier. These theories emphasise the need for respect for persons and for taking seriously the rights of individuals. Certainly it is a morally unacceptable proposition that one person can in all circumstances decide upon the continuation of another person's existence, and the source of disquiet here is the lack of respect for the autonomy of the individual so manifested. It is important to appreciate why the idea of autonomy plays such a central role in theories which emphasise respect for persons. For these theories go beyond the purely practical point that the best way to discover the values believed in by any person is to leave the decision to that person. This view is something which certain forms of utilitarianism would readily concede, especially if it viewed all matters of moral belief and values as contingent. Autonomy theories, however, argue that humans have special moral attributes, most notably their ability to understand and act upon moral rules (the idea of self-determination). Indeed, this is what makes them 'persons'. Moreover these theories hold that moral rules must apply to everyone and we must respect everyone's right to self-determination if we concede his or her moral standing. Thus in deciding upon a person's continued existence without having regard to his own views, we infringe the most basic moral principle of respect for persons as ends in themselves.

The idea of autonomy provides us with a useful language for discussions of this sort, namely the language of rights. Rights are attributes of individuals as moral persons which cannot be overriden merely by appeals, for example, to increased social utility. Thus the ascription of a right to life would make inadmissible much utilitarian argument about the 'value' of life and the moral permissibility of taking life to reduce suffering or increase happiness.

However, although autonomy theories, and the idea of a moral right to life, may state the truth, they cannot as such state the whole truth, and the doctrine as it stands is either inadequate or incomplete. For although the idea of respect for persons provides us with a special explanation of the wrongfulness of taking of life in the case of the normal, developed adult, it is of questionable application in other situations. These cases, such as the foetus, infants, the mentally ill, and the comatose, have more direct relevance to problems in medical practice, but are the very life-forms where the paradigm conditions for autonomy do not exist, for they make no choices and are unaware of themselves as special persons.

Moreover, there may be a degree of pain and suffering involved in such life-forms and the consequence of applying autonomy theories is to commit us to maintaining life at a cost of great suffering for all concerned.

Thus, we find some writers advancing the argument that both utilitarianism and autonomy-based ethics can throw light on the problem of the value of human life.[9] What we need to note, however, are the differing reasons for valuing life and to attend to distinctions about the meaning of human life. For example, Singer draws a distinction between what he sees as two distinct meanings of 'human life'. One meaning is membership of the species homo sapiens but, argues Singer, in itself such a biological classification has no special moral significance. That we should have ever considered it to be so is probably a carry-over from the Christian doctrine of ensoulation. Secondly, what is of special moral significance is the idea of human life as a 'person', or in other words the possession of certain special characteristics, the most significant being rationality and awareness of oneself as a continuing entity. Singer's argument is that what is morally wrong about the taking of the life of a 'person' is the disrespect shown for his or her autonomy. But why should we place value on 'conscious' life, a category which would include the cases of 'mere' membership of the species homo sapiens (such as infants and foetuses) as well as animals? Ex hypothesi it cannot be because such life-forms enjoy autonomy, though in some cases it makes sense to talk of the potential for autonomy. In this category we can find good reasons for valuing merely 'conscious' life in utilitarian considerations, for these life-forms can themselves experience pain and pleasure, and the continuation or termination of their existence can lead to the increase or decrease in the happiness of others.

A similar general argument has been presented by Glover, who points to a distinction between life as 'mere' consciousness (awareness, or the having of experiences) and life at a higher level of consciousness, which includes certain emotional and cognitive experiences. This second state is of importance, in that it is an aspect of a life worth living whereas mere consciousness has no value in itself but is valuable only as a means to a worth-while life. Glover notes that there can be many proposed candidates for what

13

constitutes a life worth living and he does not attempt to list all of these (though he does stress that his concept of a life worth living is not necessarily identical with that of a morally virtuous life). But the lack of the ability to specify the ingredients of a worth-while life has some significance for Glover's general argument, for he is led on to argue that the best judge of the worth of a life, at least as regards the continuation of that life, is the person living it; or in other words, the crucial criterion here is that of autonomy.

Thus we find Glover advancing the argument that, whereas the only relevant moral considerations in cases of 'mere' life are those based on consequences or side-effects, in the case of worth-while lives there are direct reasons for not killing, that is reasons based on the particular life itself (or the person whose life it is).

We should make clear a distinction to be drawn in claims based on autonomy which stress the need to allow a worth-while life to continue or develop. These arguments need not pre-suppose any particular form of the good life (such as may have been argued for in ancient philosophy). Some theories do perhaps point to a particular form of life as the good form but use the argument from the necessary incompleteness of knowledge or from relativism to argue that these are matters for the individual. What such theories are saying, accordingly, is that although there may be such things as morally good life-styles, there is a practical difficulty in knowing precisely what these are, and that the value of autonomy is that it leaves decisions as to what is morally good to the person or persons directly concerned. However, other theories look to autonomy as necessarily a central feature of moral life; these take the value of autonomy as something independent of the particular type of life which the autonomous person chooses. In other words, autonomy is itself a moral good, and is to be treated as such.

We can then note the general argument about the value of human life. Simply as life, there are good reasons for respecting life, such as the capacity to feel pain (and pleasure) enjoyed by the particular life-form, the possible and actual contribution of that life-form to general social welfare, and other considerations of a similar utilitarian nature. But because of the possession of certain crucial moral characteristics human life has a special value over and above its value as 'mere' life. Of course, this argument so far has lacked substance, for there has been no attempt to show how we should then value the lives of say foetuses or animals. Rather the concern has been with explaining the sort of considerations which will be used in later chapters applying the principle of sanctity of life to consideration of some of the problem cases encountered in medical practice.[10]

Showing disrespect for human life.

In the next few chapters we shall be applying this discussion of the value of life to a number of more concrete examples. However, before concluding this discussion of the general idea of the sanctity of life, we must take note of different ways of showing disrespect for human life. The preceding discussion enables us to understand what is involved in the moral assessment of the taking of life. The paradigm case of showing disrespect for human life is murder, that is the intentional killing of another human being. What is wrong about murder is not so much the side-effects or appeals to utilitarian considerations (which may have little force where the victim suffers little pain and the murder is undiscovered) but its failure to take proper regard of the victim's autonomy. However we should note that although murder is the most obvious mode of not respecting a persons's autonomy, because of its preconditions of intentionally injurious conduct for which the fullest moral responsibility follows, it is not the only way in which death can be said to result from human action for which responsibility can sensibly be attached.

Consider, for example, the case of the man who drowns while able swimmers watch on or the biblical account of the man helped by the Samaritan but whom the priest and the Levite passed by. Now it is certainly true that legal systems vary to the extent to which omissions are punishable at criminal law but no system punishes omissions in the same way as positive actions. But the fact that the law, on the whole, refuses to punish failures to act in the same way as it punishes positive acts does not in itself show that morality does or ought to make a similar distinction between omissions and acts. There are reasons peculiar to the law itself, such as the practical difficulty of specifying which particular omissions should attract legal liability and which should not, which make the punishment of omissions particularly problematic. It is not necessarily the case that moral systems face the same difficulties in identifying particular situations as ones which lead to moral responsibility.

The doctrine of acts and omissions, according to which moral responsibility is appropriate in cases of positive actings but only very rarely if at all in the case of omissions, is often invoked in the debate on euthanasia. However it is a doctrine increasingly questioned. Yet it is the idea of negative acts or omissions, and the responsibility for not acting or for allowing things to happen, which is relevant to the sort of case where a doctor refuses to treat newly-born deformed babies or the terminally ill.[11]

Moreover such issues have relevance for a general discussion of the doctrine of sanctity of life for they act as a reminder of the variety of ways in which responsibility for the loss of life can arise. In Great Britain, more than 6,000 people are killed in road accidents every year.[12] Now these deaths are not simply unavoidable in the way that deaths from ageing (decline in the body's capacity to reproduce cells) are unavoidable, for there is a way known to us now to prevent these deaths, namely by banning the motor car. (It should also be remembered that such figures are not just bare statistics but state the total deaths of actual people.) Similarly thousands of people are killed or injured every year at work. Again, it is within our power to prevent these deaths and injuries, by insisting upon higher standards of safety at work, or by prohibiting certain industrial practices (e.g. coal-mining). Another point is that it cannot be said that these deaths are the result of people voluntarily undertaking the risks of driving motor cars, in the way for example that people accept the risks of inherently dangerous activities such as mountaineering. Several studies have shown that few people have any awareness of the risks which are part of everyday life, whether at home, in the factory or on the roads.[13]

However, few people who profess a belief in the sanctity and value of life would be prepared to argue for the prohibition of motor-vehicles or the dismantling of industry as a matter of moral duty. No doubt the reason is that the deliberate taking of life (as in murder, or more problematically abortion) is a greater moral evil than allowing the continuation of motor-car 'accidents'. However, each results in the ending of life. The point must be stressed: we can save over 6,000 lives every year by taking the step of banning the motor-car.

The reason we do not do so derives partly from our refusal to accept or ascribe moral responsibility for anything but deliberate (and usually positive) actions. However, this view depends to some extent on accepting the emphasis placed by Christian belief on conscience and intentional conduct. But it is surely wrong to deny moral responsibility for letting continue a state of affairs, which we know as a matter of fact has such fatal results. Further the lack of support for any campaign against industry and the motor-vehicle (to remain with our two examples, though there are many more) also derives from the fact that we arrange our values in such a way that the value of life is put well below that of social wealth or economic efficiency (both of which would be threatened by the removal of motor-cars or industry).

Similarly, the way in which resources are allocated will indicate the true value placed on life by society, or more accurately by those who have the power to make decisions on these matters.[14] For instance, it is clearly possible, simply as a matter of fact, that in the U.K. dialysis machines could be provided for every kidney patient requiring one. Yet we as a society do not do so, because we do not want to pay higher taxes or because we prefer to spend money on different things (e.g. nuclear weapons). Again what is happening is that we do not allocate social resources in such a way as to have the effect of preventing deaths. An even more startling illustration is the case of persons who die from hypothermia. One of the causes of these deaths is the appalling social conditions (especially housing) in which most of the victims live. Yet there is nothing necessary or unavoidable about bad housing conditions: we could relatively easily provide suitable housing for all persons at risk from hypothermia. But in the full knowledge that the present allocation of resources has the effect that each year many people, most of them elderly, die of hypothermia, we continue to accept the situation and thereby give an indication of the extent to which we take seriously the idea that life is sacred.

The present discussion has shown that the idea of the value of life is a complex one, and its application in different circumstances will be examined in the following chapters. However the important point is that discussion of these issues should be direct and open and that the sort of decisions which such theoretical reflections are meant to inform should similarly be made directly and explicitly. Yet our present means of allocating social resources points to an implicit disvaluing of life of people like motor-car victims or the aged. Perhaps such people are indeed candidates for euthanasia, or perhaps their lives should be disvalued (though it is difficult to see what possible moral criteria there could be for such views) but if so it would be better to admit what in fact happens.

NOTES

1.   Schweitzer, A., Reverence for Life, cited by Glover, J.,
      Causing Death and Saving Lives, Harmondsworth, Penguin Books,
      1977, at p. 39.

2.   Schweitzer, A., Civilization and Ethics, cited by Singer, P.,
      Practical Ethics, Cambridge University Press, 1979, at p. 91.

3.   Singer, op.cit., at pp.91-2.

4.   For discussion of some of the problems, see Leake, R.E., 'Live
      Animal Studies' in McLean, S.A.M., (ed), Legal Issues in
      Medicine, Aldershot, Gower Publishing Co., 1981, pp. 53-66.

5.   Illich, I., Limits to Medicine. Medical Nemesis: The
      Expropriation of Health, Harmondsworth, Penguin Books, 1977
      edition, especially at pp. 70-85. For further discussion of
      Illich, see chapter 10, infra.

6.   See infra, chapter 6.

7.   For discussion of the general issues in the euthanasia debate,
      see infra, chapter 3. Particular problems concerning the
      termination of medical treatment are discussed in chapter 4,
      infra.

8.   This doctrine is discussed in Glover, op.cit., chapter 4. See
      also, chapter 4, infra.

9.   Singer, op.cit., chapter 4, especially at pp. 72-81; Glover,
      op.cit., chapters 3-8.

10. See chapters 2-4, infra.

11. On the principle of acts and omissions, see further chapters 3 and 4, infra. It is worth noting here the famous lines in Arthur Hugh Clough's The Latest Decalogue:

> 'Thou shalt not kill; but need'st not strive
> Officiously to keep alive.'

These are frequently, but mistakenly, invoked in the debate on active and passive euthanasia. In fact, the target of Clough's satire was the hypocrisy of a society which claimed to hold a belief in the sanctity of life, while at the same time acquiescing in a social structure which disvalued, and indeed shortened, the lives of many people in it.

12. The figures for the period 1976-1980 are as follows:

1976	6,570
1977	6,614
1978	6,831
1979	6,352
1980	6,010

Department of Transport; Scottish Development Department; Welsh Office, Road Accidents in Great Britain, H.M.S.O., 1981.

13. On this point, see Atiyah, P.S., Accidents, Compensation and the Law, London, Weidenfeld and Nicolson, (3rd. Ed.), 1980, chapter 5.

14. For the argument that allocation of medical resources involves social and political considerations, see infra, chapter 10.

2 Abortion

We noted earlier that medical practitioners look to both law and
morals as sources of guidance for their actions. It should be borne
in mind, however, that morality contains different and competing
positions and the law on certain matters is not always clear and may
also vary in content from one legal system to another. Even when
morals and the law give a clear position the guidance provided by each
may well differ even to the extent of conflicting, and a good
illustration of these various points is the case of abortion.
Abortion is certainly a topic that has been considered by moral
philosophers for centuries and is also one of the classical cases
considered by medical ethics. Yet very little attention has been
given (especially by philosophers) to the discussion of what the law
of abortion should be as an issue separate from the morality of
abortion, though the more practically-oriented medical ethics has
looked to the difficulties encountered by doctors and nurses when
confronted with legal rules which conflict with their moral beliefs.
Thus although some theorists have written about the special problems
in legally permitting or prohibiting abortion,[1] this topic has
received very little attention when contrasted with such issues as the
moral status of the foetus or the rights of the mother to have control
over her body.

In one sense this general position is surprising, for the issue
of the relationship between law and morals, and the particular issue
of whether the law should be used to enforce morality, has been
discussed in depth by legal philosophers. However, it is important
to keep distinct the interest of the fields of law and morality in

abortion (though this is not to say that these are necessarily separate in every respect) as these relate to medical practice on abortion. Although the positions on abortion adopted by the law and morals may differ and any such difference should be noted, we should also remember that when we are considering the question of what _ought_ the law to be (in contrast to what the law is) one central consideration for this question is the moral position on abortion.

The Morality of Abortion.

1.   When does human life begin?

One obvious issue of relevance in considering the moral issue of abortion is that of showing when the life of a human being can be said to begin.   The reason for this point of inquiry being raised is the belief that, if we grant the premise that (all other things being equal) it is wrong to take human life, then if we can also show that at certain stages of development there is or is not human life, abortion is correspondingly impermissible or alternatively permissible.   But it must be said at once that there appears to be little of practical value to be gained from this way of tackling the abortion issue from the perspective of morality, for if the issue is what sort of 'human' state do we value, then this can be stated more directly in terms of the value of life as discussed in chapter 1. This conclusion may come as something of a surprise, for the issue of when life can be said to begin has certainly dominated the literature on abortion.   Yet there are difficulties with all of the proposed candidates for the point at which this moment occurs.   Some of these difficulties relate to the fact that the criteria for ascertaining the beginning of life do not provide us with a clear-cut point in making this determination.   Another problem is that even where there is a relatively distinct point, its moral significance is not always apparent.

Take for instance the idea which was for long believed, and which historically had some influence on the development of the law, that there was a 'separate' human life at the moment of quickening, i.e. when the mother first feels the foetus move.   However, it is impossible to understand what moral significance this stage has, for the arrival of the stage at which the foetus moves is not significant in terms of its physical development. It may well be that the importance attached to quickening derives from its supposed (but false) connection with the stage of viability, another stage which it is argued has moral significance. Viability is reached when the foetus has developed to the stage at which it could live on its own if separated from the womb. Here at least we can perceive reasons for taking this point as being relevant to the issue of abortion, for in one sense a viable foetus is a separate being from that of the mother.

The importance attached to the stage of viability has influenced the law. In England and Wales it is an offence to destroy a child capable of being born alive (Infant Life (Preservation) Act 1929, which was not amended by the Abortion Act 1967). In the case of Roe v. Wade,[2] the Supreme Court of the United States decided that the American Constitution gave a woman a right to privacy which encompassed her decision whether or not to terminate her pregnancy. However, the Court also declared that the right was not absolute and that the law could regulate the conditions for abortions between the end of the first trimester (or three months) of the pregnancy and the stage of viability, and moreover once viability has been reached that the law could prohibit abortions altogether, except those necessary to preserve the life or health of the mother.

But wherein lies the significance of the stage of viability? A viable foetus, like the new-born child, is still dependent upon others for its continued existence, even if no longer necessarily dependent on the mother. Yet if it is permissible to abort the non-viable foetus because it depends upon the mother, why is it not also permissible to take the life of a viable foetus, which also must be dependent upon other people? Contrariwise, if it is wrong to kill a viable foetus (or a newly born child) why should it be permissible to abort a non-viable foetus, the only difference between the two cases being the identity of the parties upon whom the foetus is dependent. Also as Glover points out many people (e.g. old people) are in some way dependent upon others, but this feature can hardly be thought to justify the taking of these lives.[3] It should also be borne in mind that the stage at which viability is reached depends upon the extent of medical knowledge and technology necessary to maintain the life of the foetus.   It seems odd to use a stage so dependent upon the purely varying and contingent factor of the availability of medical aid as a morally crucial boundary, unless viabilty has some other significance.

Two other stages which have featured in the debate about the beginning of life are those of conception and birth.   The argument that birth is the morally significant step in the beginning of human life is usually advanced by pro-abortionists.   However, it is difficult to see what the crucial difference is between the newly-born baby and the foetus immediately prior to birth;   the only biological difference is that one is located outside the womb, the other within it.   But why should this be morally significant?   Certainly it is an advantage of this criterion that it presents us with a sharp and easily identifiable boundary, but this fact is hardly of great note if it possesses no further moral significance.   There is also the problem of showing why, if it is permissible to take the life of a foetus at any stage of development, it is not also permissible to take the life of a newly born child.   Simply to use the stage of birth as the appropriate cut-off point gives us no reason for discriminating between the moral propriety (or impropriety) of abortion and infanticide.

The argument which makes the moment of conception crucial in setting the marking-off of human life is subscribed to by many because this is the stage adopted by the Catholic Church (on the basis that from the moment of conception there may be, rather than always is, a soul), but the argument has an independent secular basis.   Most importantly it is argued that in biological terms the development of a human from a single-cell zygote, (i.e. at conception when there is a single-cell of 23 pairs of chromosomes, one in each pair taken from each parent) to a multi-cell zygote and conceptus, to an embryo (when it develops what visibly looks like human features), to a foetus, to a newly-born baby, is a continuous process with no sharp and stark divisions.   Moreover, there is the view that at the moment of conception there is a unique being with a specific genetic make-up which makes this moment of crucial importance.[4]

But there are difficulties in taking conception as the point of moral significance.   One is that the zygote is so unlike anything which we would normally recognise as a human being.   It is true that we must take the zygote as a potential human being, but that is a different matter. We would not wish to associate the features of an oak-tree with the acorn, though we know that the acorn is a potential oak-tree. And any argument about destroying potential, as opposed to actual, human beings raises questions about the morality of contraception, the purpose of which is the deliberate prevention of the development of (potential) human life.[5] We should also note that certain forms of contraception used at present involve the destruction by rejection of fertilised eggs.

When we look at the range of arguments, then, it appears that if we are looking for a significant 'stage' in the development of human life, of the stages examined here the most significant is that of conception. But we should remind ourselves that such significance derives mainly from the biological argument about the nature of the growth of life. As such this biological argument is unassailable but we should also note that what we are searching for is a stage which has _moral_ significance and should remind ourselves of the argument about the different meanings of human life and the different considerations involved in valuing such life. It has been noted that there is a distinction between human life as 'mere' life and human life as characteristic of a person, i.e. the possession of morally relevant characteristics. The foetus or the human at earlier stages of development, even that of conception, can certainly be described as a life-form, but it is clearly begging the question to state that the special considerations appropriate to moral persons necessarily apply to the zygote or to the foetus.

2.   The argument from rights.

There is another form in which the argument on abortion is sometimes stated, and that is in the language of rights. However, it will be argued that, just as much of the discussion on identifying the boundaries of human life is not directly relevant to the central moral issue, similarly the language of rights is not the most appropriate mode of locating the issues.

It should be stressed that what we are concerned with here are moral rather than legal rights. We shall see later that in terms of the Abortion Act, strictly speaking no legal rights as such are given to the foetus or to the mother, nor indeed to any other person directly involved in the pregnancy, for example the father. However, the moral rights typically taken as of relevance to the issue are those said to be enjoyed by the mother and by the foetus. Usually the rights of the mother are stressed by those favouring abortion on general feminist grounds, and the most basic right in these terms is that of complete control by the mother over her own body, a right that would encompass the decision to reject the unborn child at any time while it is located in the womb. On the other hand those seeking to show that abortion is morally wrong tend to invoke the right of the unborn child (usually ascribed to the foetus) to be born. However, we can see at once the difficulty about stating the problem in this way, for a simple statement of the various competing rights shows that there is no obvious way of balancing or choosing between them without going on to discuss the more substantive moral issues. Furthermore, some of the arguments for the ascription of rights to women or foetuses are in themselves questionable.

An influential paper which uses the idea of a woman's right to control her own body is that presented by Thomson,[6] who claims not to deny absolutely that the foetus may have a right to life. Rather her view is that nothing in any such right to life entails the right of the foetus to use the body of the mother. We should note one significant feature about this mode of stating the issue, namely that the priority given to the woman's right to control her body only contingently leads to the overriding of the foetus's right to life as in the present state of medical science it is not possible to maintain the lives of foetuses unless the removal from the womb is at a relatively late stage. If, however, foetuses could be 'extracted' from the womb at any stage and kept alive by other means, then both the rights of the mother and of the foetus could be satisfied. On that basis abortion (the taking of the life of the foetus) would lack justification.

The basis of Thomson's argument is that we need to note the different ways in which it can be said that one ought to do something. It is only when one can be said to be under a duty to do (or not to do) something that it makes sense to talk of the right of another that it is done (or not done). Thus A's duty not to murder B is the correlative of B's right not to be murdered by A. But a duty to do something is for Thomson to be contrasted with what one ought to do merely in the sense that it would be a good thing to do. (Consider the actions of the Good Samaritan, who did the right thing though under no duty to do so). Thomson argues that the mother's right to control her body overrides the foetus's right to life unless it can be shown that the mother has a duty to let the foetus remain in her womb (rather than this being a good thing to do). But the criterion which she suggests for this duty is that of the degree of responsibility of the mother for getting pregnant, and the nearest we find to a duty on the mother's part to keep the foetus in her womb is where the pregnancy was willing and no good reason has in the interim arisen for not continuing it ('good' being independent of the mere whim of the mother). But this argument is odd, for some duties (as in the case of the duty not to murder) are owed to everyone, irrespective of any special relationship with the person to whom the duty is owed.

Thomson backs up her argument with a separate point that the mother's right is overriding because she 'owns' her body and has the right to expel anyone from it. But apart from the general oddity of seeing moral rights in terms of legal notions like ownership, this argument does not succeed. Both at law and in morals, there is no reason to suppose that owners of property have complete control over it. Indeed there is a large literature on the topic which reinforces the view that property rights are subject to general social control. In most modern legal systems, property owners are increasingly put under duties to persons on their property, even trespassers (who may be expelled from the property by the owner, but may not lawfully be killed or injured in doing so).

The strongest case for an appeal to the rights of the mother is the right of self-defence, i.e. the mother has the right to abort the foetus where the continuation of the pregnancy will threaten her health or may even result in her death. This right in itself would not allow abortion in all cases, but only in those where it can be shown that the mother's health or life is indeed under threat. However, the right to self-defence arises in specific situations which should be distinguished from others, and that is where the attacker is intending to kill the victim. It is the evil intent on the part of the assailant which explains the moral permissibility of self-defence. But the situation is different where a person is placed in circumstances where he must choose between his own life and that of another and that other has no injurious intentions (in other words the applicable defence is that of necessity rather than self-defence). The defence of necessity is not as clear-cut in application as that of self-defence, but it is difficult to see how the issues involved are made any clearer by stating them in the language of rights.

An argument using rights but moving in a different direction is that which stresses the rights of the foetus. Here the most important right is that of the right of the foetus to be born. An objection to this argument may be that there is something in the nature of moral rights such that it does not make sense to ascribe moral rights to foetuses. Certainly we should note that the law confers various rights in respect of injuries incurred and benefits conferred before birth, and even conception, of the persons concerned.[7] However, while in one sense law does give rights to the foetus, the crucial point about these legal rights is that they are dependent upon the person being born alive and have no effect if there is no birth.

Feinberg[8] points out that although the legal position may lend some support to the idea that it makes sense conceptually speaking to ascribe rights to foetuses, it hardly provides an argument for ascribing a right to be born, as the stage of birth is the crucial one in the right having effect. Feinberg favours an idea of rights relating to the interests of the right-holder (an alternative approach is to emphasise the benefits accruing to someone said to have a right), but he argues that there is no depriving of any actual interests or benefits by the foetus not being born. At most the foetus can have future interests or future benefits but again these do not become actual until birth. Feinberg continues to argue that the only way such future interests can be affected prior to birth is where the foetus's most basic interests would be destroyed if it were later to be born (e.g., it is grossly deformed). Thus, he concludes, the only right which we can ascribe to a foetus qua foetus, that is apart from those which follow upon its being born, is a right not to be born where the chances of fulfilling its interests after birth are destroyed or substantially reduced. We should note that in the

United States there have been several legal cases where the basis of the case was wrongfully allowing the baby to be born (or to be conceived at all). More recently, a similar case was raised, unsuccessfully, in the United Kingdom.[9]

3. The rights and wrongs of abortion.

Rather than argue about the 'rights' of the mother and the foetus, or when a human being's 'life' begins, it is better to confront the substantive moral issues directly. In the chapter on sanctity of life it was argued that there was a crucial distinction as regards the value of life between human life simply as a type of life-form and human life as possessing morally relevant properties (which allow for the ascription of autonomy). Now it is clear that the foetus as such does not possess those qualities associated with autonomy, such as self-awareness and rationality. What then are the appropriate factors in assessing the morality of abortion, that is the termination of the life of the foetus? One argument following utilitarian theories derives from the capacity of the foetus, given the development of its nervous system, to feel pleasure and pain, but in itself this argument does not carry much weight. A stronger utilitarian-based argument may be located in the fact that the foetus may be the source of 'happiness' (for whatever reason) to other people, such as the mother or family, and that this happiness is a reason against abortion. Equally, such utilitarian views would permit abortion where the birth of the foetus would not add to the happiness of anyone else or would increase overall pain and suffering. A different argument relates to the fact that the foetus is (or can be) a potential person. It is important to be clear that the potential qualities of persons are not (yet) actually possessed by the foetus, and so there is no room for autonomy-based arguments in a direct form. But the fact that moral autonomy does have an independent value gives us a reason for valuing the life of the foetus, for the foetus has such moral potential. To some extent, however, this consideration involves calculations as to the chances becoming actual.

This point involves calculations about the unknown, and certainty on these issues would require a greater knowledge of both medical and social science than is available at present. But these are matters on which we do find views being expressed, and it is as well to remind ourselves of the various factors appealed to in doing so. There are general considerations of relevance to this issue. One is that if the prevention of a development which would result in moral autonomy is a bad thing, then it would appear that sterilisation and contraception are also bad for that reason unless it can be shown that abortion is in some way morally distinguishable from these other practices.[10] There is a certain consistency in maintaining that abortion and contraception are both morally wrong, for each has the effect of preventing the development of morally autonomous life. However it is usually thought that there is a distinction between the two practices and that abortion should not be seen simply as a late form of contraception. The difference between contraception and abortion lies in what is involved in the different means used by each to bring about the same end of preventing autonomous life. For contraception does this by preventing the process of development of autonomous life from starting at all, whereas abortion involves the taking of a life-form in the shape of the foetus. On this view, the foetus is nearer to moral autonomy than is whatever 'life' is frustrated by non-conception. It follows from this distinction between contraception and abortion that even if both are morally wrong, abortion is more wrong than contraception, and if our aim is to prevent autonomous life it is better to do so by contraception than by abortion. The position is often adopted that, all other things being equal, abortion is unjustifiable where pregnancy could have been avoided in the first place. It should be noted that some legal systems which generally do not permit abortion, do so where the pregnancy is the result of rape for the reason that the woman is not responsible for becoming pregnant.

Furthermore there are arguments about the dangers of over-population, which would weigh against seeking to maximise human autonomy in the sense that every opportunity should be taken to add to the numbers of human beings, but these arguments lend more support to contraception than to abortion.

One significant point which should be stressed is that the onus of the argument tends to lie on those seeking to kill a foetus, and this is not dependent solely on the relatively weak point that the

foetus has capacity to feel pain.   The basic idea here is that it is
a good thing that there are persons with moral autonomy, and we should
not take steps to prevent this, at least where there is already a
life-form which has potential for moral autonomy.   At the same time,
we can point to particular cases where we can state with a good degree
of certainty that there is little likelihood of the foetus achieving
moral autonomy later in life.   Examples would be where there are
gross mental, or perhaps physical, disabilities.   But it must be
emphasised that many types of handicap do not preclude a meaningful
life (and this goes beyond moral autonomy), and history abounds with
examples of people who have struggled with success against severe
disabilities.   So to some extent there should be caution in asserting
that because a child will if born be handicapped then abortion is
justified.   We need to be sure about the nature and extent of the
disabilities.

The crucial point about this argument concerns the assessment
of the chances of the foetus developing moral autonomy in later
life.   As such, this approach would render impermissible abortions
carried out solely to maintain the mother's figure or to prevent the
cancellation of holidays scheduled for the time of birth, both of
these being instances which have featured in the literature on
abortion.   Two objections may be made against this relatively
restrictive position that abortion is justifiable only where there is
little chance of the foetus achieving potential as a morally
autonomous person.   The first objection is that to restrict the
permissibility of abortion in this way is to frustrate the moral
autonomy of the mother for she is deprived of a choice which affects
her life in cases where she wants an abortion for reasons other than
lack of potential autonomy in the foetus.   But it is no part of the
idea of autonomy that it permits the overriding of the autonomy of
others.   No disrespect is shown for the person of the mother by
denying abortion in these cases unless it can be shown that she should
not be held responsible for becoming pregnant.

A second objection states that questions about the expected
'quality' of life, and not simply potential autonomy, of the foetus
are relevant to deciding upon abortion.   However, it should not be
thought that questions about the meaning of moral autonomy are
completely independent of the issue about the quality of future

life. In some cases (e.g. gross deformity or extreme poverty) matters which appear to relate to quality of life may have some bearing upon deciding what is meant by an autonomous life which should be valued as such.

One final point to be noted is that the argument so far justifies abortion in certain circumstances, namely where we feel sure that there is no potential autonomy possessed by the foetus and arguments about the quality of life may be of relevance in determining this. An objection to this argument is to show that these considerations could equally apply to the case of young children who have actually been born, and also certain other cases (such as the aged or the mentally ill). This may indeed be the case, but the proper conclusion to draw is that the morality of infanticide and other forms of euthanasia calls for re-examination.[11]

Abortion and the Law.

One point which has been mentioned already, but which bears repetition at this stage, is that the functions of law and morality do not necessarily coincide (and certainly their contents at times differ). The discussion so far presented in this chapter has been to the effect that there are circumstances in which abortion can be taken as morally justifiable, but that not all cases of abortion can be so justified. What implications does this view have for the legal regulation of abortion?

Somewhat surprisingly much theoretical discussion stops at the issue of the moral propriety or impropriety of abortion, and does not go on to discuss the relationship between the morality and law of abortion. This is surprising because philosophers have for some time argued about the legal enforcement of morals.[12] Admittedly the case of abortion is different in some respects from the issues which featured in the debate, such as homosexuality and drug-taking. For some of the proponents of the legal enforcement of morals were using the term morals in the sense of the feelings and beliefs actually felt in a particular community as opposed to morals in the sense of the rational assessment of such feelings and beliefs. But it is not clear what, if any, consistent view is held as a matter of fact in a community on the issue of abortion. Certainly in a society like the United Kingdom, which draws upon different religious and moral traditions, it would be surprising if there was one commonly held view. Another point is that in much of the discussion on enforcing morality by means of the law, the examples appealed to involved so-called victimless crimes. But it would simply be begging the question to state blandly that abortion is a victimless activity, for there is need for argument about the appropriate moral status of the foetus.

However, it is clearly not the case that the moral argument covers the position which should be adopted by the law in respect of abortion, for there are factors which are relevant to deciding what the law should be which are out of place in considering the morality of abortion. One of these is that not only do some women want to have abortions, but many will have them whether or not abortion is legally permitted. Legal prohibition in such circumstances may have several deleterious effects. One is the danger to the health of the woman seeking the abortion, a danger which might result in death. Another is the labelling as criminal of people involved in a situation which differs in many respects from what is normally thought to be criminal conduct. Accordingly, there may well be reasons for not legislating against abortion even in cases where we would say that abortion is morally wrong.

However, there are two arguments advanced which seek to dismiss these practical concerns of the law as irrelevant, and which instead support the idea that the law should enforce the morally proper views on abortion. One such argument is that the law is not a neutral social institution but plays an important part in expressing social values. Accordingly the law, by prohibiting abortion, should express the value of life, even if such a law cannot be enforced. But against this it should be noted that it is not the general value of life which is being expressed, but rather the value of those life-forms threatened by (legalised) abortions. So this argument does not depend upon any claim that the law, by permitting abortion, shows disrespect for human life generally, as the category of the foetus is a distinct one and can be perceived as such. In other words, permitting abortions is not necessarily a step on the slippery slope. Another point is that the persons who most need to be

32

'reminded' of the value of life expressed by the law are precisely those who will in any case disobey the law, unless it can be shown that the prohibition of abortion by the law does have some deterrent effect.

A second argument against legally permitting abortion, even in cases where this is to be condemned morally, rests on the idea that if the law does not condemn a practice such as abortion then it is condoning it. Interestingly, this argument has been advanced in other areas of morals where changes in the law have been discussed.[13] For example it has been argued that if the law permitted homosexuality, even between consenting adults, then it would be seen as condoning what some people thought to be a thoroughly immoral practice. This argument became a live legal issue in R. v. Knuller(Publishing,etc.)Ltd.[14] After reforms in the law by the Sexual Offences Act 1967 had removed the illegality of certain homosexual practices, a charge of conspiracy to corrupt public morals was brought against the directors of a magazine which had published advertisements inviting readers to meet the advertisers for purpose of homosexual practices. The House of Lords held that although the activities in question were no longer illegal they could still be thought to corrupt public morals. Lord Reid stated:

> I find nothing in the Act to indicate that Parliament thought or intended to lay down that indulgence in these practices is not corrupting. I read the Act as saying that, even though it may be corrupting, if people choose to corrupt themselves in this way that is their affair and the law will not interfere.[15]

And Lord Morris of Borth-y-Gest added:

> What section 1 of the Act does is to provide that certain acts which previously were criminal offences should no longer be criminal offences. But that does not mean that it is not open to a jury to say that to assist or to encourage persons to take part in such acts may be to corrupt them.[16]

What follows from these considerations is that the issue of the moral propriety or impropriety of abortion is one, but is not the only, factor relevant to deciding upon the question of what the law about abortion ought to be. It is important to bear in mind both the possible interaction of law and morals as well as their differences in aim and methods when considering how actual legal systems deal with abortion.

Legal regulation of abortion.

There are a variety of positions which the law can adopt in respect of abortion. These range from the extreme of absolute prohibition to that of abortion on request (i.e. the right of the mother to insist upon therapeutic abortion without giving any reason for this and irrespective of the stage of the pregnancy). There are a number of intermediate positions including

1.   prohibition except where necessary to save the mother's life
2.   prohibition except where necessary to save the mother's health (which may be defined on strictly medical grounds or alternatively on sociomedical factors)
3.   permission where the child will suffer from some defect, defined on either medical or sociomedical grounds.

Other variations relate to the stage of the pregnancy (e.g. abortion not being permitted after the 28th week) or the cause of the pregnancy (e.g. as a result of rape or incestuous intercourse). The Report of the Lane Committee on the working of the Abortion Act[17] gives a brief summary of abortion laws throughout the world. The most remarkable aspect is the degree of variation of these laws. Certainly there are far more countries which forbid abortion absolutely than allow it on request (which is permitted only in some socialist states). Most countries do allow abortion on the ground of saving the mother's life or health, and others allow social factors to be considered in deciding upon this matter.

In Great Britain the most significant part of the law on abortion is the Abortion Act 1967. However, it is not possible to ignore other aspects of the law for the effect of the 1967 Act is to remove the existing prohibitions on abortion in certain specified conditions. Prior to the Act it was an offence for any person to supply a woman with means of carrying out abortion, and for any person to administer any poison or noxious thing with the intent to procure the miscarriage of a pregnant woman (Offences against the Person Act 1861, sections 58 and 59). However, in the case of R. v. Bourne[18] it was held that an offence was committed under the 1861 Act only when the accused acted 'unlawfully' and that this did not occur when a doctor acted in good faith for the purpose of preserving the life of the mother. A further Act, the Infant Life (Preservation) Act 1929, created the offence of wilful destruction of a child capable of being born alive (prima facie proof of which is that the pregnancy has proceeded beyond the 28th week). The Lane Committee noted that the effect of these Acts, and their interpretation in case-law, was to give the law a degree of imprecision, which affected the medical profession as to when and when not abortion was permissible. This state of affairs was similar in Scotland, where neither the 1861 Act nor the 1929 Act applies and it is unclear whether the rule in R. v. Bourne had a Scottish counterpart. In fact, abortions carried out in the exercise of responsible medical judgment were never prosecuted but this was a consequence of the policy of the Crown Office not to prosecute rather than of a clear statement of the law.

The effect of the 1967 Act is to permit abortion in certain circumstances, but where these do not obtain, the previous law continues to apply. Abortion is permissible under the Act when it is carried out by a registered medical practitioner if two registered medical practitioners are of the opinion, formed in good faith, that continuing the pregnancy would involve greater risk than terminating it:

1   to the life of the mother, or
2.   of injury to the mother's physical or mental health, or
3.   of injury to the physical or mental health of any existing children in the family.

An abortion is similarly justified where two practitioners are of the opinion that there is a substantial risk that the child would suffer from such physical or mental abnormalities as to be seriously handicapped. The Act provides that when doctors are determining the risk involved in continuation of the pregnancy, they may take account of the mother's actual or reasonably foreseeable environment. An abortion under the Act must be carried out in a hospital or nursing home which is either part of the N.H.S. or is approved by the Secretary of State. It is worth stressing that the grounds for abortion under the Act are 'medical' in the sense that they relate to the risk to life or health in the continuation of the pregnancy, even although environmental factors may be taken into account in determining this risk. The Medical Termination of Pregnancy Bill, which later became the 1967 Act, in its original draft did contain a so-called 'social' clause, which provided that a pregnancy could be terminated if the pregnant woman's capacity as a mother would be severely strained by the care of a child (or another child). However, this clause was not enacted into law. Despite this, it is sometimes thought that the Act does allow abortion on 'social' grounds as something separate from abortion on 'medical' grounds. Thus, the Lane Committee noted, in discussing section 1(2) of the Act:

> But there is no doubt that, as the critics point out, the subsection is regarded by many people within, as well as outside, the medical profession as meaning that an undesirable environmental situation of the mother of itself suffices to justify abortion.[19]

However, the Committee took the view that the intention of Parliament was that abortion was to be permissible only on 'medical' grounds, though environmental factors are relevant to these, and not on 'social' grounds. They accordingly reached the opinion that the wording of the Act laying down the criteria be left unamended. More recently, controversy has arisen about an abortion notification form issued by the D.H.S.S. which requires the surgeon carrying out an abortion under the Act to specify the medical condition justifying the termination of the pregnancy. It has been argued that such a form is restrictive of the law in not allowing abortion on 'social' grounds, but in fact it is the Act itself which permits abortion only on medical grounds.

In cases of emergency where the doctor decides to carry out the abortion in the opinion that to do so is immediately necessary to save the life or prevent grave injury to the pregnant woman's health he may do so without obtaining a second opinion. A final point is that the Act explicitly covers the case of conscientious objection to participating in abortions under the Act by providing that no person may come under a legal duty to participate in any treatment authorised by the Act to which he has a conscientious objection except in cases of necessity.

It should be noted that the 1929 Act does not apply to Scotland as it was thought that the crime of concealment of pregnancy would cover similar cases. However, the development of modern techniques of therapeutic abortion has had the effect that as long as the provisions of the 1967 Act are complied with abortion in Scots law may be carried out no matter how far advanced the pregnancy is.

Several points should be noted about the way in which the 1967 Act regulates abortion. Although the legal system does allow a child rights to protect interests relating to events prior to its conception or birth, these rights are ineffective until the child is born alive. There is nothing in the 1967 Act to suggest that the child has any legally recognised right to be born (or indeed not to be born). Neither is the father of the child given any role in the decision on abortion. In the case of Paton v. Trustess of BPAS,[20] a woman had consulted two registered medical practitioners, who formed the opinion that the continuance of her pregnancy would involve risk of injury to her physical or mental health and that she could have an abortion under the 1967 Act. Her husband, who was the father of the child, had not been consulted by either his wife or the doctors on this matter. He claimed that he had a right to have a say in the destiny of the child and sought an injunction to prevent the abortion being carried out without his consent. The court, however, held that the husband had no right in law to prevent the abortion. It should be noted that Parliament refused to accept an amendment to the Medical Termination of Pregnancy Bill that abortions of married women under the Bill should be dependent upon obtaining the consent of the husband.[21]

But we should also note that if the 1967 Act gives no rights to the foetus or to the father, it gives none to the mother either. The position was described in Paton in the following terms:

> The two doctors have given a certificate. It is not and cannot be suggested that that certificate was given in other than good faith and it seems to be that there is the end of the matter in English law. The 1967 Abortion Act gives no right to a father to be consulted in respect of the termination of a pregnancy. True, it gives no right

to the mother either, but obviously the mother is going to
be right at the heart of the matter consulting with the
doctors if they are to arrive at a decision in good faith,
unless, of course, she is mentally incapacitated or is
physically incapacitated (unable to make any decision or
give any help) as, for example, in consequence of an
accident.[22]

Thus under the 1967 Act the woman has no right to an abortion
even if her case objectively conforms to the requirements of section
1. Her entitlement to abortion depends rather upon two medical
practitioners actually reaching the opinion that her case is covered
by the Act. Indeed the Act itself gives the woman no right _not_ to
have an abortion. Thus doctors who act in pursuance of the 1967 Act
would not infringe the law on abortion if they carried out an abortion
where the woman had not given her consent or was unwilling. However,
such cases would almost always be covered by the law relating to
assault, which is actionable at both criminal and civil law.[23]

The crucial role in operating the scheme under the 1967 Act is
that of the medical practitioners. In the case of R. v. Smith(John)
it was said:

> The Act, though it renders lawful abortions that before
> its enactment would have been unlawful, does not depart
> from the basic principle of the common law as declared in
> R v. Bourne[1939] 1 K.B. 687, namely, that the legality of
> an abortion depends upon the opinion of the doctor. It
> has introduced the safeguard of the two opinions: but, if
> they are formed in good faith by the time the operation is
> undertaken, the abortion is lawful. Thus a great social
> responsibility is firmly placed by the law upon the
> shoulders of the medical profession.[24]
> (Emphasis added)

In Paton the judge referred to this passage and added the comment that
'it would be quite impossible for the courts in any event to supervise
the operation of the 1967 Act'.[25]

In practice, therefore, the complex ethical and legal issues
involved in abortion have become dependent for their resolution on the
workings of the medical profession (which in this context includes the
nursing profession[26]). This factor has some significance for
understanding the operation of the Abortion Act. Although the Act
uses a strictly medical model, and presents the issues as medical in
nature to be decided on by the medical profession, it is not at all

clear that the medical aspects of abortion can be so easily isolated from general social and moral aspects.[27]

One final point to note about the Abortion Act is that, as was argued earlier, even if it allows for abortions of dubious moral propriety, the Act may still be justified if it contributes to the solution of various social problems. In this context the success of the Act may in part be reflected by the statistics relating to illegitimate births, deaths through illegal abortions, and the number of illegal abortions.

The chief difficulty with this exercise is that either we do not have the appropriate data, or if we do it is not possible to show a causal link with the Abortion Act. Thus, Hart, writing in 1972 of the first three years operation of the Act, stated that the Act had succeeded in securing a substantial reduction in the number of illegitimate births, but admitted that there may well be other explanations for this trend.[28] Although the figures for deaths from illegal abortions show a decrease since the passing of the Act, this trend was in any event in progress prior to the passing of the Act, and problems about the statistical method of recording maternal deaths from abortion influence the interpretation of the available figures.[29]

A reduction in the number of illegal abortions was said to be one of the principal aims of the Abortion Act, but in attempting to measure this we encounter almost insuperable problems, lacking as we do any reliable data on the numbers of illegal abortions prior to and after the passing of the Act, or even convincing methods of calculating such figures. The Lane Committee[30] reached the conclusion that the Act had made a real contribution to a reduction in the number of illegal abortions, but this was stated in a very tentative way and has since been challenged.[31]

In short, the 'success' of the Abortion Act in solving social problems, independent of ethical arguments about the permissibility of abortion, is still to a great extent unknown, and requires considerable improvement in gathering and interpreting the relevant data before we can begin to answer this part of the abortion question.

NOTES

1. Brody, B.A., 'Abortion and the Law', (1971) 68 Journal of Philosophy, 357.

2. 410 U.S. 113 (1973).

3. Glover, J., Causing Death and Saving Lives, Harmondsworth, Penguin Books, 1977, at pp. 124-5.

4. Finnis, J., 'The Rights and Wrongs of Abortion', (1972) 2 Philosophy and Public Affairs, 117, 145.

5. For further discussion of aspects of contraception, see infra, chapter 7.

6. Thomson, J.J., 'A Defense of Abortion', (1971) 1 Philosophy and Public Affairs, 47. Thomson's argument is discussed by Glover, op.cit., chapter 10.

7. Some of these issues are discussed in McLean, S.A.M., 'Ante-Natal Injuries', in McLean, S.A.M., (ed), Legal Issues in Medicine, Aldershot, Gower Publishing Co., 1981, 150.

8. Feinberg, J., 'Is There a Right to be Born?', in Feinberg, Rights, Justice, and the Bounds of Liberty, New Jersey, Princeton University Press, 1980, 207.

9. The English case is McKay v. Essex Area Health Authority & Anor., 'The Times' 20 February 1982. The American cases are discussed in Note, 'A Cause of Action for "Wrongful Life": A Suggested Analysis' (1970) 55 Minnesota Law Review 1.

10. See further chapter 7, infra.

11. See further, chapters 3 and 4 infra.

12. The so-called Hart-Devlin debate. See Devlin, P., The Enforcement of Morals, London, O.U.P., 1965: Hart, H.L.A., Law, Liberty and Morality, London, O.U.P., 1963.

13. For example, the note of reservation to the Report of the Committee on Homosexual Offences and Prostitution, Cmnd. 247/1957, at pp. 117-121, discussed and criticised by Hart, H.L.A., The Morality of the Criminal Law, Jerusalem, The Hebrew University Press, 1965, at pp. 43-8.

14. [1973] A.C. 435.

15. at p. 457.

16. at p. 460.

17. Cmnd. 5579/1974, vol. I, pp. 219-224.

18.   [1939] 1 K.B. 687.

19.   Cmnd. 5579/1974, para. 203.   On this point, see also Hart, H.L.A. 'Abortion Law Reform: The English Experience', (1972) 8 Melbourne University Law Review, 388, 393.

20.   [1979] Q.B. 276.

21.   See Bradley, D.C., (1978) 41 Modern Law Review, 365, at p. 368.

22.   [1979] Q.B. at p. 281.

23.   On consent, see chapter 5, infra; and on actions against doctors on the grounds of assault, see chapter 8, infra.

24.   [1973] 1 W.L.R. 1510, at p. 1512.

25.   [1979] Q.B. at p. 281.

26.   In Royal College of Nursing of the United Kingdom v. D.H.S.S. [1981] A.C. 800, the House of Lords held that a termination of pregnancy was within the meaning of section 1(1) of the 1967 Act where the treatment was prescribed and initiated by a registered medical practitioner, but was actually carried out by qualified nursing staff acting in accordance with his directions.

27.   See further, chapter 10, infra.

28.   Hart, (1972), loc.cit., at pp. 401-2.   Hart strengthens this point by noting the decrease in the rate of illegitimate births per live births over the period 1968-1970.   However, it should be noted that since the time of Hart's paper, there has been a steady increase in this rate, as well as an increase in the overall number of illegitimate births: see O.P.C.S., Population Trends No. 26, (1981), Table 9.

29.   Cavadino, P., 'Illegal Abortions and the Abortion Act' (1976) 16 British Journal Criminology, 63, at p. 64.

30.   Cmnd. 5579/1974, vol. I, Section Q.

31.   Cavadino, loc.cit., at p. 63.

3 Euthanasia

In many ways the subject of euthanasia follows on from that of abortion, for there is a substantial overlap between the central issues of abortion (when if at all it is right to take the life of a foetus) and of euthanasia, which is concerned with the moral propriety of a course of action which results in someone else's death. But we should also note that there are differences between some of the arguments surrounding abortion and euthanasia. The chief among these is the emphasis given to the idea that if euthanasia is to be justified at all, it must be for the good of the person to be killed, whereas in the abortion debate the well-being of persons other than the foetus is allotted a fairly direct role. This is, however, simply one aspect of the euthanasia debate, and does not necessarily constitute a major difference between the two issues. Moreover, it is also worth noting that the sort of idea which runs throughout the issue of euthanasia is to be found also in the Abortion Act 1967. One of the points which doctors must consider when deciding whether a pregnancy should be terminated is whether there is a substantial risk that if the child were to be born it would suffer a degree of physical or mental abnormality such as to be seriously handicapped (1967 Act, section 1(1)(b)). One commentator has stated that this part of the law authorises ante-natal euthanasia.[1]

There is a further significant difference between abortion and euthanasia which should be mentioned at once. It was noted earlier that although some countries prohibit abortion absolutely, most legal systems do permit it under varying conditions. However, euthanasia or mercy-killing is not explicitly recognised as legally permissible anywhere (though legal systems do vary in the sort of liability which follows in cases of mercy-killing and the type of punishment usually given in these cases).[2]   It is all the more surprising, therefore, to discover that euthanasia, at least in certain forms, is allegedly a not infrequent occurrence in modern medical practice.   Even this view is not without challenge, however.   One writer has argued that because of the control of acute infective illnesses and the development of artificial cardio-respiratory support systems, there has arisen a 'furor therapeuticus', a drive to maintain life irrespective of the quality of the life that is being maintained.[3] But against this it has been asserted that whatever the legal position, euthanasia is something we already have in fact and it is stated to be medical practice not to adopt all life-prolonging procedures or medications where it is felt that the condition of the patient is such that the effect would be merely to delay death by an insignificant time-scale at the cost of prolonging pain.   One important aspect of current medical practice is that many doctors admit to practicing euthanasia, at least in a passive as opposed to an active form, and it is also believed that such passive euthanasia is permitted by medical ethics and (though this is not so clear) even by the law.

Euthanasia and terminal care.

Before we consider the main moral issues involved in euthanasia, we must deal with a further preliminary issue which arises from the fundamental point already stated that euthanasia is generally thought to be justified if it is done for the good of the person who dies. One objection to any sort of euthanasia is that death, when this is a result of a decision not to prolong life or to keep alive, can never be for the good of the patient.   Rather what we should do is to maintain the life of the patient so that even in cases of terminal illness our proper concern is with the promotion and practice of terminal care.   The main idea underlying this objection to euthanasia is that it is morally preferable to make the last days of a patient as comfortable and painless as possible rather than to cause or accelerate death in any way.

The problem about taking terminal care as a total substitute for euthanasia is that as a matter of fact we cannot at present alleviate pain in all cases of terminal illness. In these cases, if our aim is to make dying as little distressing and uncomfortable for the patient as we can, a better course of action may be to speed along the stage of death and in so doing eliminate pain and distress. Furthermore, it is not at all obvious that the purpose of medical treatment is simply that of alleviation of pain, irrespective of the effect of such treatment on the type of existence encountered by the patient. Certainly if it were possible that death could be postponed indefinitely or that all pain could be alleviated, then it might make sense to use all means to prolong life, but such a state of affairs is not obviously desirable and in any case it is not a reflection of the current situation.

Types and means of euthanasia.

Much of the debate on euthanasia uses a number of distinctions which must now be noted and discussed. One distinction relates to the 'means' used in carrying out euthanasia, namely active and passive euthanasia, and this is discussed shortly. A second important distinction relates to the categories of euthanasia, which for this purpose is divided into voluntary, involuntary and non-voluntary euthanasia. The basis of this division is to be found in the existence or otherwise of a request by the patient that euthanasia should be carried out. In the case of voluntary euthanasia the patient, in the exercise of a meaningful choice on the matter, has actually consented to euthanasia. Involuntary euthanasia is where the patient has capacity to decide but has either not been consulted on the matter or has stated that he does not want euthanasia to be carried out on him. To be contrasted with both of these is non-voluntary euthanasia; here the patient is unable to make any (meaningful) choice as to whether or not euthanasia is to be carried out and so simply cannot express his consent (examples include foetuses, infants, severely mentally ill and the permanently comatose).

i. Involuntary euthanasia. The case of involuntary euthanasia illustrates many of the issues involved in euthanasia generally. What is morally improper about taking the life of someone who has expressed his wish to live or who has not been consulted although he has capacity to make such a choice? On one version of utilitarianism there is nothing intrinsically wrong about this. Indeed it could be argued on this basis that even if euthanasia was clearly a bad thing for the person killed, it might still on balance be thought morally good because his death leads to increased social happiness or cuts social costs. But it is precisely examples of such reasoning which are used to point out the weaknesses in such forms of crude utilitarianism.[4]

But is involuntary euthanasia wrong if we can show that in fact death is for the good of the patient? Utilitarian theorists find it difficult to say 'yes' to this question, except in terms of the rather imprecise bad consequences, such as the threat to feelings of security, to which any practice of involuntary euthanasia may give rise. The source of moral condemnation of involuntary euthanasia is to be found rather in consideration of autonomy-based ethics. For in the case of involuntary euthanasia, we are proposing to take the life of someone who has moral autonomy, and has therefore the capacity to express his wishes as to his own death and may have expressed his wish not to be killed. To continue with euthanasia in such circumstances is to override the autonomy of that person, and differs from the case of murder, if at all, only in that death is for the good of the person killed. A crucial point to stress about arguments from autonomy, and one which is recognised in current medical practice is the significance of acting only at the patient's consent.[5] To disregard this factor is to disregard the patient as a moral agent, for the whole idea of autonomy is that decisions about a person are for that person himself to make.

ii. Voluntary euthanasia. In moral theory the case of voluntary euthanasia is likewise relatively clear-cut. Indeed it might be thought that most of the problems in this case are practical ones, but even these are in principle superable and it is this category of euthanasia which has been at the centre of attempts to legalise euthanasia. Voluntary euthanasia would appear to be supported by arguments from the autonomy of the patient, for in such cases the patient has given his consent. Moreover there appears to be little moral difference between voluntary euthanasia and suicide, except that in the former the agent causing the death is someone other than the person who is killed (and in Scotland, unlike England, there is no crime of aiding and abetting suicide). So why should there be any objection to voluntary euthanasia?

One argument is that we have no right to decide that we should die, and that suicide is equally as wrong as consenting that someone else should take one's life. In other words the right to decide upon our own death does not follow from our right to life. Now there is nothing necessarily absurd about the general notion that we can enjoy rights such that we have no option to waive their application (an example often cited in this connection is the right to education). Thus some rights co-exist with duties on the part of the right-holder in respect of the same subject-matter. But it is not clear that the right to life should be taken as such a non-waivable right.

The traditional religious prohibition against suicide rested in the belief that the decision as to the time of death was not for humans to make at all, but was God's prerogative. But this sort of reasoning is totally out of place in any system of secular ethics, and it is worth noting that in many countries the legal prohibitions against suicide have been removed in recent years.

However, even if we do permit suicide, the permissibility of voluntary euthanasia may not follow. In other words, the right each of us has to decide upon our own death does not necessarily relieve other people of their duty not to take our life. Nevertheless, in the context of the relationship between doctor and patient, it is not obvious that if we allow that the patient has the right to decide upon his own death, his expression of his wish that the doctor take steps to bring this about should give way to the normal duty of the doctor not to take life. Indeed it would appear that refusing to act upon the request of a patient in such circumstances would be to frustrate his moral autonomy. (A further point about voluntary euthanasia is that there need not be any harmful side-effects given the requirement that the patient must consent to the euthanasia.)

Underlying many objections to cases of voluntary euthanasia (and also suicide) is the view that we may have doubts about the genuineness of the patient's request to die. At one level this is an argument solely about the side-effects of the practice and can be met by insisting upon exacting procedures for the giving of consent (e.g. that it must be in writing and witnessed, that death should not follow immediately upon giving it to avoid the request being a temporary reaction to pain or depression, and so on). Alternatively, it may be argued that by definition no one can freely and truly consent to their own death, for to prefer death to continued existence cannot be the result of a rational choice, no matter the prospects for that continued existence.[6] The main difficulty about this is that it is contradicted not only at the level of intuition, for it is not obvious that life is preferable to death in every set of circumstances, but also in that it is in conflict with medical practice in some terminal cases.

iii. Non-voluntary euthanasia. * The category of non-voluntary euthanasia is probably that category which causes the most pertinent problems in current medical practice. Euthanasia can be said to be non-voluntary where the patient lacks the capacity to know or to express his wishes as to his continued existence. Such cases would include infants, the permanently comatose and severe instances of mental illness. These cases are examples of the idea of human life as a 'mere' life-form as contrasted with human life as moral agency and the difficulty they pose stems exactly from the fact that it is not possible to ascribe autonomy in such instances.[7]

It might be thought that if arguments about respect for the autonomy of persons have no place, then such problems can be resolved relatively simply by making a utilitarian calculation as to the pains and pleasures of the continuation of the life-form in question. In one sense this is true but it should not be thought that such a calculation would be straightforward. To a great extent the issue is whether life can be continued in such a way that it still bears some value. So arguments about the quality of life are crucial here. Certainly, there appears to be little point in continuing to let remain 'alive' persons who will never regain consciousness, and whose existence depends solely upon life-support machines. Likewise, there are some cases where handicaps, either physical or mental, are so severe (and, importantly, permanent) that there seems to be little or no value in such a life. Something like this approach is embodied in

47

section 1 of the Abortion Act 1967 which was mentioned earlier. It is a point worthy of note that when doctors are considering this aspect of the decision as to whether a pregnancy should be terminated they are not required to have consideration of the environment of the mother or family, factors which are appropriate when deciding upon other grounds for abortion. Rather the sole issue is the type and degree of handicap of the child itself if it were to be born.

One of the difficulties in making any decision as to non-voluntary euthanasia is knowing all the relevant factors to consider. Certainly it should not be thought that just any physical or mental handicap makes a life worthless; the handicap must rather be very severe for this consequence to follow. These problems stem from the fact that the most important moral perspective on deciding the issue is lacking, namely that of the person directly affected by the decision. One way of dealing with this difficulty is to conduct a thought-experiment along the following lines. Imagine we have a sense of what a normal life is like in the sense of possessing rationality and self-awareness, and have all the relevant medical knowledge about the types of illnesses and handicaps which might prevent development of capacities associated with moral autonomy. We are then told that we have to change our lives to one whereby we do suffer some form of handicap or illness. The crucial question then becomes, in what cases, if any, would we choose not to be alive rather than having such a handicapped life. Clearly, if we thought that the handicap was not permanent in nature, we would not opt for non-existence, and this would probably also be true even if there was a degree of pain during the occurrence of the handicap. Similarly, the loss of some faculties or limbs (e.g. blindness) would scarcely decrease the value of life to such an extent that death or non-existence would be preferable. Nor would all impairment of mental faculties have such an effect. But once we reach the stage where there are severe physical or mental handicaps, then such a continued existence would not be preferable to death. These severe conditions need not always have the result of preventing the development of those mental faculties associated with moral autonomy but could also relate to circumstances of physical handicaps (e.g. continued dependence on a machine and complete lack of mobility) where we would prefer no existence to existence of that particular type.

However, we have to distinguish here cases where severe physical handicap affects someone who has already moral autonomy and continues to have it. In such cases only voluntary euthanasia is possible. But there are also instances of handicaps of this sort as a feature of the development of life-forms which have not yet attained autonomy (e.g. foetuses, infants).

Whether or not there can be complete agreement about the outcome of such a mode of deciding on when euthanasia is justified, this procedure has the advantage of stressing the link with the idea that euthanasia is for that person's own good, for what we are trying to capture by resort to such reasoning is some conception of what that type of life would be like and whether it would be preferred to no existence at all. But often we find in discussion on euthanasia that the attitudes and wishes of others (such as parents) are taken into account. However, we should not judge such considerations totally out of place. It should be remembered that in many cases of non-voluntary euthanasia the handicaps or abnormalities are such that it is unlikely that moral autonomy can ever be predicated (again) of that life, the main exception to this being the case of the (normal) foetus, which involves the separate argument of the potential for autonomy.[8] But utilitarian-based considerations are surely in order here if we are to talk at all of the values of such life. For instance, it does not seem a morally improper factor when deciding not to use or to continue to use treatment on those who are permanently comatose to look at the cost (including alternative deployment) of such treatment. It should not be thought that such arguments about side-effects will always point to the use of euthanasia, for there are indeed many cases where families have felt their own lives enriched by looking after severely handicapped children. But against this it must also be borne in mind that the cost of trying to cope with severely disabled children or retarded relatives may be too much for many families. Again it should also be remembered that other people (e.g. those wishing to adopt children) may be able to manage in such circumstances. However, when we are dealing with such cases where it is known that moral autonomy of the life will not be achieved, is there any point in continuing such a life when no one else (either family, friends or society generally) gains from that life or wishes it to continue?

This type of argument may appear to result in conclusions which are too harsh. But the thought-experiment above may give us reason to re-consider any conclusion such as this. For included in the factors to be considered when deciding on the value of life are various facts about the society in which the life would be spent. This would include the likelihood of being cared for by a loving family, or if rejected by the family, the type of care and concern shown by other social agencies. And depending upon the sort of society in which we are to live, it might well be that the combination of physical handicap plus rejection or stigma by society (such as is said to exist in the case of the mentally ill or the aged) might not be preferable to death. One reason why we might not apply as much weight to social factors as to medical knowledge in this thought-experiment is that we feel that there is a greater chance that social views and attitudes may or can change (e.g. a society could decide to invest more in the care of the handicapped). But if we wish to use this thought-experiment to lead to practical outcomes then we must take into account the way in which our society actually does treat such cases as the handicapped and the aged, and if these are factors which tell against the value of life we need also to calculate the likelihood of improvements in that society's attitudes and allocation of resources. It is one thing for a society to profess a belief in the value of even a handicapped life, but another to put this belief into practical effect. If we have to decide upon euthanasia for those unable to make their own decision it is proper to consider actual social practices.

Active and passive euthanasia.

There is a further important distinction which features in the euthanasia debate; this relates not to the different categories of euthanasia but rather to the means employed in carrying it out. In particular a distinction is drawn between active and passive euthanasia. Active euthanasia occurs whenever steps are taken which result in death where death would not have occurred without those steps. Passive euthanasia occurs where there is a failure to use available measures and this failure leads to death which would have

50

been avoided or postponed by their use. It must be stated at once that the importance of this distinction lies not so much in any moral difference between these two modes of euthanasia, for any such moral difference is both questionable and is increasingly being questioned, but instead in the fact that whereas active euthanasia is explicitly repudiated by the medical profession, some doctors admit to practising passive euthanasia, at least in the sense that in certain cases they do not take all possible steps to maintain life. Further, although this point is not clear, it may be that the legal effect of not acting with the consequence that death occurs is less serious than actively taking life. It may indeed be because of this supposed legal doctrine that medical practitioners adhere to their views on the distinction between active and passive euthanasia. But a mere statement that something is accepted medical or legal practice provides nothing by way of moral justification, and it is to that point we must now turn.

One doctrine which has been adduced to give support to the distinction between active and passive euthanasia is the doctrine of acts and omissions, whereby there is a morally relevant difference between doing something on the one hand and on the other refraining from doing something else which has identical consequences.[9] But merely as a distinction between different ways of describing action this has no obvious moral relevance. If our object is to cause death, why should it be thought less bad merely to let a person die than to take steps to kill him, when the consequences of the action either as positive act or negative omission are the same? A different mode of appealing to this doctrine is to say that there is a moral difference between doing and omitting to do in that in most cases we have negative duties (that is not to do certain things) but we are only rarely under a duty to take positive steps. Thus it might be thought that it is clear that we ought not to push someone into a river but that it would be a matter of supererogation rather than duty to jump in and save a drowning man.

But we must be clear what we mean about duty in such cases. Certainly, the law does not punish failure to act in the same way as it punishes harmful acts. However, this is because of the lack of precision in formulating a clear statement of the law rather than a reflection of any moral distinction. For it is not obvious that the able swimmer who refuses to rescue someone who is in danger of drowning is in an entirely different situation from the person who pushes another into water, since the intended or foreseen consequence (namely the death of the other) may be the same in both cases.

Furthermore the locating of appropriate duty as a way of explaining the moral difference between acts and omissions does not necessarily solve the problem when considered from the perspective of medical practice. For the issue then becomes what are the appropriate duties owed to patients who are, for example, terminally ill. It is not clear that the duty to maintain life at all costs is the sole relevant one, for another is the duty to relieve pain. As Foot has pointed out these duties may conflict in the present context.[10] Indeed passive euthanasia may result in the breach of the duty to relieve pain. Take, for example, the case of a cancer patient whose condition is so severe that extreme pain can be avoided only by giving such high doses of pain-killers as to shorten life and in effect to 'actively' kill him. It scarcely seems right that the appropriate thing to do is to refuse to give pain-killers but instead passively allow the patient to die in pain. Another case mentioned by Rachels is that of the severely disordered Down's syndrome new born baby whose death results from the refusal to operate to remove intestinal obstructions.[11] He notes that this death would be a relatively long-drawn out and painful process, yet if our intention is that the child should die then the most humanitarian thing to do would be to give it a lethal injection. It is difficult to see why passively standing by and allowing death to happen should be thought morally less blameworthy than actively taking steps to speed up the time of death. Indeed the reverse seems to be true.

It is a point worthy of note that the ethics of the Catholic Church, which adopts on the whole a strict view of the sanctity of life, would permit the administering of pain-killing drugs even though the consequences would be to shorten life, by an application of the doctrine of double effect. According to this doctrine, in certain circumstances, where the intention behind an action is good, the action is permissible even although it is known that undesirable consequences will also follow.[12] In the present context, then, double effect would allow the giving of lethal drugs, so long as the intention is to alleviate pain rather than to accelerate death.

Although double effect correctly identifies the role of intention in the assessment of moral responsibility, it is questionable whether this assessment can be made without any regard to the consequences of action. In any case, there are difficulties in putting the idea of double effect into practice, for there is no way of knowing simply from the action of injecting pain-killers, whether the resulting death was the intended aim of the action or was instead an unwanted but inevitable consequence of seeking to relieve pain. Indeed it is sometimes claimed that the use of passive as opposed to active euthanasia is justified on this more practical ground of the difficulty of inferring intention from action.

A variant of the acts and omissions doctrine is the argument that in certain cases there is a duty to treat only by way of ordinary means but that extraordinary means need not be used. This view is accepted by the Catholic Church in its acceptance of the distinction between proportionate/disproportionate means, and is probably also adopted in medical practice.[13] Further, the argument might be thought to embody the distinction between duty and supererogation. However, there is a practical difficulty in applying this argument, and this is that the distinction between ordinary and extraordinary means is not at all a clear-cut one. The idea that treatment is ordinary or not would seem to depend upon both the state of medical technology (either that actually available in a particular case or that which could have been available given a different allocation of medical resources) and the condition of the patient. But even if we can make this distinction in particular cases, what moral relevance has it in the context of the doctor-patient relationship? If the doctor's duty is that of maintaining life at all costs, why should he not be under an obligation to do so by using all available facilities, whether ordinary or not? On the other hand, if the doctor can justifiably refuse to apply treatment to a patient where its effect would be to maintain life, why should this be restricted only to so-called extraordinary cases? Again the central issue appears to be that of what are the actual duties of the doctor in treating the terminally ill or the handicapped, not how such cases are to be treated.

Law and Euthanasia.

In marked contrast to the case of abortion, which is permitted to varying extents in many legal systems, no legal system explicitly allows for euthanasia in the form even of (so-called) mercy-killing by doctors on patients who have expressed their consent. Any such action will render the doctor liable to criminal prosecution. We should note however that in the United Kingdom bills to legalise voluntary euthanasia were presented to Parliament in 1936, 1950 and 1969 but were not enacted into law. These bills all contained provisions seeking to ensure that the request of the patient was truly voluntary. The society EXIT still seeks to promote the legalisation of voluntary euthanasia but there is no obvious sign of popular support for this move. It should also be noted that certain States in the U.S.A. have enacted so-called allowing-to-die legalisation, the best known of these being the Natural Death Act of California. The effect of this legislation is to relieve doctors of any legal liability for refusing to treat various cases where the patient had previously made a directive concerning his own terminal care.[14]

However, the general position in law is that euthanasia is forbidden. In those legal systems in the common law tradition, the attitude of the law is that so long as an accused person had the intention to kill (or knowledge that death would result from his actions), his motives for so doing are irrelevant. In short the law treats euthanasia as murder. A slightly different approach is taken by those legal systems of the civilian tradition where mercy-killing is still treated as illegal homicide but the motive such as to relieve pain or acting on the victim's consent is recognised as a mitigating circumstance. But even here the effect of the law is that euthanasia still leads to legal liability and punishment, though to a lesser degree.

However, there are important qualifications to this formal position of the law which must be noted. The first of these is that for there to be unlawful killing the acts of the doctor must have caused the death of the patient, and the somewhat elastic nature of the idea of causation has enabled courts to avoid convicting doctors who have participated in mercy-killing. Thus, where the patient has died as a result of himself taking drugs supplied by others, then the offence here is that of aiding and abetting a suicide (although this is not a crime in some countries, such as Scotland). Furthermore, the law at times resorts to something like the position of double effect when a patient has died as a result of the administration of pain-killing drugs. In the case of R. v. Adams,[15] the judge (Devlin, J.) directed the jury that when a doctor administered drugs to relieve the pain in hopeless cases, even if it could be proved that the drug shortened the patient's life, this was not a cause of the death in the legal sense; the cause of death was rather the illness from which the patient had been suffering.

Yet another point to bear in mind about legal liability for euthanasia is that only very rarely will there be liability where there has been a failure to act. In such circumstances the prosecution must show that there was a duty on the doctor to take some action, and in practice prosecutions will rarely be brought when death has resulted from failure to act whatever the theoretical position about the proper duties of doctors may be. It is this practice of the law as much as anything that probably accounts for the acceptance by the medical professions of passive as opposed to active euthanasia. This point leads to one final matter about the law of murder and the practice of euthanasia and that is that no matter what the law in the books may say, the law as it is actually administered is another matter. Williams[16] has listed a number of factors in this connection, such as

1. the difficulty of proving requisite guilty intention, especially in cases against doctors
2. the reluctance of prosecutors to proceed against doctors who have acted in good faith (and the prosecutor's discretion on this matter may be unchallengeable)
3. the reluctance of the jury to convict in cases of mercy-killing even when the evidence is very strong
4. the passing of relatively lenient sentences where there is a conviction.

Given this picture of the law and euthanasia in both theory and practice, the question arises whether we should change the law. One argument often used against any change is that for the law explicitly to allow the taking of human life would be the beginning of a very slippery slope, which may well start with genuine examples of mercy-killing but could easily end up with widespread non-voluntary euthanasia being practised for political, social or racial motives.[17] Very often the example of the Nazi euthanasia programme is used to support this view, for it is said that the Nazi programme itself was initially intended to cover only true cases of relief of incurable suffering, but quickly degenerated into horrible and massive genocide. However we have to be careful about what exactly did cause the murder of so many innocent victims by the Nazis. It would appear to be a better historical explanation to view the cause of the genocide as being the beliefs of the Nazis, rather than the mere fact that euthanasia was permitted in certain restricted cases. What is really at issue is whether permitting euthanasia in certain circumstances would necessarily lead to attitudes or programmes like those of the Nazis. It is unlikely that in itself euthanasia would encourage beliefs such as racial superiority and political intolerance, or that the rise of political movements which supported racism would be held in check by maintaining the prohibition on voluntary euthanasia. Moreover, as the attitude of many humans towards animals illustrates, it is a feature of moral practice to compartmentalise our thinking, and there is no reason to believe that the move from the taking of the lives of those who request it or who are terminally ill, to the taking of the lives of political opponents, would be at all a likely step.[18]

One problem about accepting the present state of the law is that the gap between what the law prescribes and what actually happens is so great that there is social hypocrisy on a grand scale. At present the position is that, through the formal position of the law, we profess the view that euthanasia of any sort is on a par with any sort of murder. However, in practice, by a variety of means, not all cases of killing are prosecuted as illegal homicide and we seem to accept medical practice as determinative of the issues. This view has indeed been urged as a proper one. For example, in his illuminating study Meyers presents a strong case for the recognition that euthanasia in certain circumstances is morally proper and concludes his argument by stating[19]:

In the last analysis, it is submitted, without specific changes in the criminal law codes, we must trust to the professional ethics and humanitarian motives of our physicians to guide them in choosing how far and what nature of treatment shall be pursued in the particular circumstances of a given case.

Similarly, the Archbishop of Canterbury in discussing literature on the proposals to legalise euthanasia said: 'The warnings given in these books seem to me to be so weighty as to make the case very strong indeed for leaving the issues much as they now are in the hands of doctors'.[20]   But this situation is far from satisfactory.   For one thing it does not provide doctors with immunity from prosecution, even in those cases where doctors act in accordance with accepted professional practice.   Such immunity can be brought about only by prosecutors firmly adhering to a policy not to prosecute in particular cases, but the prosecutor's discretion on this matter may not be an absolute one and he may be forced to initiate prosecutions as a result of pressure from outside organisations. Further, the possibility of private prosecution could not be avoided by this tactic.

Another difficulty is that medical practice itself depends as much on what the law is perceived to be as on understanding of the ethics of euthanasia, as the use of the highly questionable distinction between active and passive euthanasia in medical ethics would seem to suggest.

There is also the more substantive problem that allowing the practice of the law to deviate from the statement of the law is nothing other than a refusal to face moral problems directly.   If, in fact, we think that certain types of euthanasia (such as voluntary euthanasia or non-voluntary euthanasia in cases of severely handicapped newly-born babies) are not morally improper and we manifest this belief in a system where those who practice such types of euthanasia are not prosecuted, why should the law continue to treat such cases, even theoretically, as murder?   Indeed there lurks an even more profound problem about the present situation, namely that the difficult and perplexing questions about the propriety of euthanasia are left mainly if not entirely in the hands of the medical profession, yet such matters are scarcely those that call for medical expertise for their resolution.[21]

NOTES

1. Davis, B., 'The Legalization of Therapeutic Abortion' 1968 S.L.T. (News) 205, at p. 207.

2. It has been argued that the laws of Switzerland and Uruguay come near to the position of permitting euthanasia, but in neither case is euthanasia or mercy-killing totally free from legal liability. See further, Meyers, D.W., The Human Body and the Law, Edinburgh University Press, 1970, at p. 155.

3. Nicholson, R., 'Should the patient be allowed to die?' (1975) 1 J. Medical Ethics 5.

4. For further discussion, see supra, chapter 1 at pp. 9-11.

5. On the place of consent in medical practice, see chapter 5 infra.

6. Compare the notion of 'pious perjury' used in the old law when suicide was a crime entailing certain legal and religious consequences, that to avoid these consequences it was deemed that the suicide must have been insane at the time of his death, and hence not responsible. However, this was explicitly a legal fiction.

7. See supra, chapter 1 at pp. 13-15.

8. See supra, chapter 2 at pp. 28-31, and infra chapter 4 at p. 65.

9. This doctrine is discussed by Glover, J., Causing Death and Saving Lives, Harmondsworth, Penguin Books, 1977, chapter 7. See also chapter 4 infra.

10. Foot, P., 'Euthanasia' (1976) 6 Philosophy and Public Affairs 85, at pp. 103-4.

11. Rachels, J., 'Active and Passive Euthanasia' (1975) 292 New England J. of Medicine 78.

12. For further discussion on double effect, see Glover, op.cit., chapter 6. The formulation of the principle of double effect in the text is in accordance with that featured in most philosophical discussion. For instance Glover writes (at p. 87):
'This doctrine can be summarized crudely as saying that it is always wrong intentionally to do a bad act for the sake of good

consequences that will ensue, but that it may be permissible to do a good act in the knowledge that bad consequences will ensue. The doctrine is explained in terms of the difference between intended and foreseen consequences.'

However, it should be noted that in the principle of double effect in Catholic theology emphasis is placed on three factors in addition to the requirement that the good effect and not the evil effect is directly intended. These are (1) the action is itself good or morally indifferent; (2) the good effect is not produced by means of the evil effect; and (3) there is a proportionate reason for allowing the foreseen evil to occur.

We are grateful to Father George Donaldson of St. Peter's College, Glasgow for making this point to us.

13. See further chapter 4 infra, at pp. 63-4.

14. For discussion and criticism see Lappe, M., 'Dying while living: a critique of allowing-to-die legislation' (1978) 4 J. Medical Ethics 195.

15. [1957] Crim. L.R. 365. For discussion of this case see Hart, H.L.A., and Honore, A.M., Causation in the Law, Oxford, Clarendon Press, 1959, at pp. 308-9; Williams, G., A Textbook of Criminal Law, London, Stevens & Sons, 1978, at pp. 532-533.

16. Williams, G., The Sanctity of Life and the Criminal Law, London, Faber & Faber, 1958, at pp. 291-3.

17. For a consideration of the argument from the wedge or the slippery slope, see Williams, op.cit. (1958), at pp. 280-1; see also chapter 4 infra, at pp. 67; 74-5.

18. Kohl, M., The Morality of Killing, London, Peter Owen, 1974, at pp. 14-20; 49.

19. Meyers, op.cit., at pp. 158-9. Meyers concludes his discussion of euthanasia with the comment: 'The point at which life is no longer being preserved, but death is being prolonged, will be a tenuous and difficult one to pin-point, but it is a task for the humanity of the physician, without hindrance by overly-rigid laws.' (at p. 159).

20. Cited by Williams, Textbook of Criminal Law, p. 512n. Williams adds the comment: 'The law does not leave the issue in the hands of doctors; it treats euthanasia as murder.'

21. For discussion of the issues involved in terminating treatment,

see chapter 4 infra.   Some of the problems involved in
treating issues of euthanasia as matters for medical
decision-making are explored in chapter 10 infra, at pp. 193-4.

4 Terminating Treatment

There can be few areas where the interests of morals and the law reflect so clearly on medical practice than that area which is concerned with the withholding or withdrawing of treatment from selected groups or individuals. Since law does not always reflect morality it is likely that the views of each discipline on this matter will diverge, as may the manner in which their final decisions are reached. Indeed, both disciplines may in some situations exist to serve different ends, ends which may not coincide with the goals and aspirations of medical practice. What is clear, however, is that the development of medical expertise in the realms of treatment and diagnosis has given rise to urgent moral and legal problems. Further our views on the direction which should be taken by the law or morality in these areas may to some extent be shaped by the claims and expertise of medicine.

Thus, before sophisticated technology made the saving of life possible in situations which would previously have been regarded as hopeless, doctors (and the public) were confronted with fewer dilemmas centring on questions of life and death. The damaged baby and the elderly patient with pneumonia were in any event unlikely to survive, and medicine could do little to alter this pattern. Thus, the decision about whether or not to offer or continue treatment was largely if not totally academic. As a result of developments in pharmaceuticals and technology, the situation is now altered and the choices to be made are compounded both by the attitudes of the law and by our individual or collective views about morality. One way round this problem has been, as in the case of the brain stem dead patient, to redefine life and death (or at least death) in order to justify the withholding, or more likely the withdrawal, of treatment. The brain stem dead patient is he whose vital functions of breathing and circulation can only be maintained artificially, since those parts of his brain which control these functions have been damaged. Since brain cells do not regenerate, there is no hope of these functions being restored naturally. The patient, then, is moribund since he cannot live indefinitely even with the assistance of life-support machinery. The medical pressure to accept brain stem death as the point of death has therefore been great. There are many reasons for this, but primarily pragmatic grounds predominate. There is, we are told, no purpose in ventilating a corpse (a definition which will surely depend on the individual's view about the moment of death). Further, on the recognition of brain stem death, organs which are badly needed for transplantation purposes, can be removed.

Still another way of coping with these dilemmas has been to attempt to find moral arguments to justify our standpoint, and for most people this has involved the search for a coherent way of rationalising the fact that some people will die or may have to die in order that others may survive, or because we regard their lives as in some way less important, valuable or worthwhile in themselves.[1]

Thus, even the most apparently dogmatic commitment to life, the doctrine of the sanctity of life, is generally tailored to a more overt reflection of reality by the use of modifications.[2] There are two groups in the community, however, for whom our moral and legal attitudes in this respect are of particular importance. These are the baby born damaged and the elderly or terminally ill patient. As we shall see, although the law purports to hold a type of sanctity of life commitment in all cases of killing (bar its own exceptions of, for example, war and self-defence), its actual practical effect may be less clear and protective than might at first appear.

The Damaged Baby.

The simplest and perhaps the most emotionally appealing view to take in this area is that of the sanctity of life. The belief that life is sacred logically implies that all life, even if damaged, merits equal and total protection. One of the immediate charms of this argument is that it is overtly non-discriminatory, unlike many of those arguments which conflict with it. Fundamentally, while conflicting arguments seek reasons and bases for the moral justification of discrimination, the sanctity of life approach holds all life intrinsically valuable and therefore as meriting equal treatment.

However, as has been seen,[3] an absolute commitment to this doctrine is rare, largely because of its implications. If the sanctity of life doctrine is not coupled with, for example, the principle of double-effect or by making a distinction between acts and omissions, then we would logically be committed to a personal programme which would, by virtue of the practical impossibility of saving every life which could in theory be saved, be intolerable. Thus modification of the doctrine is evident even in those who uphold its tenets most firmly. The nature of the modifications, however, makes the doctrine less appealing than at first sight appears. For example, the principle of double-effect may in some cases permit the selection of life in a way which we have already claimed is discriminatory. Thus, if the mother requires surgery to remove a tumour and that surgery inevitably involves terminating a pregnancy, then this would be permissible, although it is evidently giving a preference to one life over another. Of course, it may be said that simply by doing nothing we are also expressing a type of preference since one life at least may be saved. But it is precisely this choice which makes this modification and that of the acts/omissions distinction less appealing. Those who favour the selective withholding of treatment, on the grounds that we are less culpable in respect of omissions than we are in respect of acts, must nonetheless (as with those who would favour active infanticide in certain cases) face the problem of drawing boundaries. That is, it will still be necessary to decide which conditions are serious enough to merit the withholding of treatment in the way that it would be necessary to decide whose treatment is to be withdrawn or who should be killed.

To this acts and omissions doctrine is also often added the application of a further test which differentiates between ordinary and extraordinary treatment. This distinction was first drawn by Pope Pius XII in a speech in 1958 on 'The Prolongation of Life'.

Given the context of the speech, it has been argued by some commentators[4] that the distinction drawn was one which had as its centre the use of sophisticated or unsophisticated technology. Thus, the decision would be a medical one based on gradation of the type of intervention to be made. However, while this distinction again has superficial charms, it nonetheless disguises certain fundamental problems.

Quite apart from the problems of drawing such technological distinctions, there remains the further problem that the decision taken may be more of a moral than a scientific nature, in which case there is no clear reason why it should be taken by doctors as seemed to be the suggestion. Thus, the decision to remove an intestinal blockage or to perform other relatively minor surgery on a Mongol baby may lead to the use of this distinction in an attempt to justify not performing it, whereas if the child was otherwise normal then we might see the intervention as perfectly ordinary. The decision, then, is not simply about matters which are capable of scientific regulation but is more fundamentally one which is tied up with other notions, such as quality of life, prognosis of improvement in health and so on.

Thus, the sanctity of life argument, with its traditional corresponding theories, can give us no clear answers to the question of life and death since implicit in this modified version is the acceptance that not all life will be allowed or helped to survive. There are of course also philosophical arguments which would exclude the principle that life is sacred and would argue that there are good reasons for infanticide which go beyond the purely practical. Essentially, these arguments are predicated on the claim that babies cannot have a right to life. For instance it has been argued that since babies have no concept of life or death, then the traditional arguments against killing do not apply (irrespective of whether the death is achieved by act or omission).[5] Life it is claimed is more than the simple biological functions of basic consciousness, breathing and so on. While these are essential to a life that is worth living, since they are the means by which other worthwhile things may be achieved, they are not in themselves intrinsically valuable. Babies, while normally in possession of consciousness have no awareness of, or desire for, life, so cannot be said to have a right to life. If it is wrong to kill only a worthwhile life, then it follows that babies are replaceable since their worthwhile life is a matter of potential. Therefore, the argument would run, even if it is wrong to kill a potentially worthwhile life, it is less wrong to do so when the alternative is a life with the same potential or greater potential for worthwhile life. This type of argument may be used to justify terminating a pregnancy where the baby is known to be damaged, on the grounds that nothing is lost if the following child is normal or has equal potential.

Another argument against killing is the so-called autonomy argument which renders it wrong to override the preference of a person for staying alive, even in circumstances where we might believe it to be in his interests not to stay alive. However, it is argued, babies do not have preferences and therefore they have no autonomy to be overridden. Babies may have desires, e.g., to be fed or changed, but this is not to be equated with a preference of life over death since it is no more that a basic instinct for survival. Thus, Glover argues[6] that there is a difference between having biological instinctive behaviour and actually having desires because, 'Desires... presuppose concepts'.[7] It is not necessary that these concepts can be verbalised, but it is necessary that they are understood and experienced by the person. The argument for personal autonomy would not therefore provide a convincing argument against infanticide.

The worthwhile life argument brings us squarely to the issue of the quality of life, a concept much employed by those seeking to support the humaneness of killing or letting die. Glover for example suggests that in the absence of a convincing reason against infanticide, and in the absence of clear criteria to determine when it may be carried out, the best alternative is for us to take decisions about the quality of life of a given child by considering whether or not we would consider such a life worth living. Not that he, or any other supporters of this line, would claim that this is an easy decision, nor would they claim that there would be a consensus readily available on which to base our decisions. Nonetheless, given our attitudes to, e.g. gross deformities, and our conviction that some forms of life are not worth living, then in their view the quality of life argument 'either ceases to be an objection to killing or else becomes a positive argument in favour of it'.[8] Thus, it is argued, the direct arguments against killing are unsatisfactory when we are talking of killing a baby. This is particularly true when we see babies as replaceable since the ultimate effect of killing will be exactly the same as the effects of not conceiving (a decision generally without moral importance), i.e. there will be one less life.

Few would take these arguments in isolation, however, since it would be disturbing to consider the implications of their routine application. Further, these types of arguments share some of the problems which we have discussed in relation to the modified sanctity of life doctrine since they also are selective, this time on the basis of age as much as of medical condition. The problem to be faced is not simply which conditions merit the application of these doctrines, but also at what stage we may reasonably be deemed to have the right to claim autonomy and therefore to have our right to life established and protected. Is it at the age of five, or ten, or twenty that we become capable of conceptualising a preference for life over death, and what would be our position up until reaching the appropriate age?

However, one attraction of accepting these arguments is that they need not apply the intellectually deceitful device of differentiating between acts and omissions[9] and therefore they could justify, if believed, the more humane practice of painless killing rather than leaving the baby to a slow and perhaps painful death. However, starkly stated, these doctrines lack the humane and emotional appeal of the sanctity of life argument which purports in its purest form to give us all the status of valuable and worthwhile citizens. For instance, those who argue for infanticide on these grounds often temper their approach by using the further doctrine of side-effects. Although there is little pretence in these arguments to a commitment to saving the life of a baby for its own sake, we are, by employing the notion of side-effects, invited to consider the effects on others of the continued existence of the damaged baby. (Interestingly, the selectivity of the doctrine becomes particularly clear here, since the effects of the continued existence of a healthy child may also be devastating, but although technically the arguments outlined above could apply to healthy as well as damaged babies, they are not in fact invoked in these cases). Thus, it is claimed that, although the death of a baby will be distressing to the parents and perhaps others, it would be more distressing had they to bring the child up. This argument is obviously based on several challengeable premises.

First, it presupposes that the distress of parents involved in bringing up a damaged baby balances equally with or overwhelms the effect on the emotional tone of the individual or the community which countenances killing of members of that community who can lay claim to legal if not moral rights. Second, it presupposes that the alternative to the death of the baby is that the parents must suffer the distress of bringing it up. Clearly, this is not the sole alternative. And third, it opens the door to a depersonalising type of choice which relates to the parents' distress rather than to other factors which might seem to be more fundamentally important. It also opens the debate to a version of the thin end of the wedge argument. This type of argument claims that once we allow A, then B (which is even more undesirable) will be less easy to preclude. This is in many cases unconvincing, and is particularly so where it depends on shifting from one group to another. For example, the argument that legalising abortion is the first step on the slippery slope to legalising compulsory euthanasia is unconvincing. However, in this case (of damaged babies) the argument applies not to shifts in groups, but rather to selection within the same group. Here it is clear that, if our decisions about which babies shall live or die are based on concepts which relate to their family or to the quality of life (which we or the family or the doctor will decide), then the potential for subjective influences and abuse is greater.

For example, our notions of the quality of life will be relative to a number of factors, and not simply to the type of life which we may feel to be supportable. Even were it possible objectively to identify what is supportable, it is likely that we will judge what is supportable on a sliding scale of possibilities which will make the worst handicaps of which we have experience those which we will choose to dispense with. Thus, we may choose to destroy or allow to die all those children who have condition X which is the most serious and unpleasant that we can imagine. Once this is achieved, however, condition Y, which did not previously seem the most serious, may then become the worst we can imagine, and so on.

It can be seen then that the arguments for infanticide have their superficial attractions, as do the arguments against it, but they have inherent problems which seem incapable of resolution without prejudicing the moral tone of society as a whole. Indeed, one strong argument against the selection of the damaged baby, or the baby with brown eyes, or whatever our choice is, to be those babies which we will kill or permit to die, is the rampant paternalism which is evident in the very making of such choices. Not only would the use of any criteria on which we could agree give rise to conceptual problems, but they would also give rise to a startling potential for abuse, evident from the crimes of the Nazis in the last world war.

However, there may be certain types of advantages which do stem from a policy which favours selective infanticide. For example, it is claimed that some defects have a percentage chance of being corrected surgically. If parents know that, were the operation unsuccessful, the baby would not be allowed to survive then they might be encouraged to take the risk of surgery thereby perhaps allowing a few more babies to survive. However, this argument presupposes that values can be placed on life which relate to the degree of normality (in itself a concept difficult to define) and simply begs rather than answers the question.

The Legal Position.

We have already seen that the legal position appears at first sight to adopt an approach which is more in sympathy with the sanctity of life doctrine than with the other possible viewpoints discussed. It was, however, also claimed that this standpoint may be less clear than it appears. Not only is it modified by the justifiable categories of homicide but it also, in general situations, adheres to the acts/omissions dichotomy and to the principle of double-effect, where applicable.

Thus, we are generally not responsible legally for our omissions. Indeed, the only situation where omissions will be equally culpable will be where there is a pre-existing duty between the person who makes the omission and the other person. In this way, parents have duties in respect of their children, and their ommissions will leave them open to criminal sanctions. Equally, and perhaps more vitally for our purposes, the doctor has a duty or set of duties which arise at the moment of offering to treat. These duties are diverse but they largely equate with the terms of his professional and ethical commitment to the saving of life and the relief of suffering. Thus, the doctor who omits to treat where there is a pre-existing duty will technically be as culpable as he who withdraws treatment. The law then does bear some similarities to one possible moral stance, even although it need not. It precludes euthanasia, for example, no matter how well motivated. Equally, the law, in giving damaged babies a right to sue for a reduction in their quality of life where this was the result of someone's negligence either before conception or before birth, seems to suggest that there is an assumption that life will continue.[10] There would be little purpose served by a right to sue if the law's position was to legitimate the termination of those lives which are damaged. Equally, it is no less a crime to kill a baby than it is to kill an adult, and although sentencing may vary, e.g. in the postpartum period, this merely reflects on the punishability of the person and not on the culpability of the act. The law therefore would seem to extend similar protections to babies, which logically implies that the act of killing them would be proscribed and that the omission to save them in some circumstances, for example in the case of parents or doctors, would be liable to the censure of the law.

Equally, the law adheres traditionally to the principle of double effect. This is most notable where the doctor selects to give substantial doses of pain-killers to a patient, knowing that the effect will be to shorten his or her life. As Mr. Justice Devlin said:

> The first purpose of medicine is the restoration of health. If this can no longer be achieved, there is still much for a doctor to do, and he is entitled to do all that is proper and necessary to relieve pain and suffering, even if the measures he takes may incidentally shorten life.[11]

This position would seem to have been reconsidered recently by the Director of Public Prosecutions who declared in a newspaper interview that 'doctors who deliberately speed death could face the prospect of life imprisonment.'[12] Were this to be the current view of the law, then there would of course be implications for the practice of medicine and its morality. As was pointed out, before this statement, 'both the medical profession and patients felt confident that doctors following accepted medical procedures would not be prosecuted'.[13]   The law's stance on the principle of double effect may seem now to be less clear.   Its position was also reviewed in two cases where there was direct consideration of the extent to which the handicapped baby requiring corrective surgery will be legally protected.

The first of these cases was that of Re B(a minor),[14] in which the parents and doctors of a handicapped baby had agreed that corrective surgery should not go ahead, with the inevitable result that the baby in question would die.   In this case, the court took the child into care and authorised the surgery to be carried out.   In the recent trial of Dr. Arthur,[15] which centred on the death of a Mongol baby requiring similar corrective surgery, some fundamental questions were raised about the practice of medicine in this area. By and large the attitude of the court was heavily dependent on the evidence of other professionals as to what they would have done in these circumstances.   Thus, the question of culpability was decided on the notion of standard or reasonable practice, a concept generally reserved for the civil rather than the criminal law.[16]   Clearly, however, since the issue in this case related to the withholding rather than the withdrawal of treatment, then the question of what the doctor's duty actually is becomes of vital importance.

To view the doctor's duty to his patient as one which can be entirely explained by his fellow professionals may be an understandable approach in some ways, but it nonetheless disguises two potentially important factors.   First it makes the assumption that the nature and extent of the doctor's duty to his patient is solely definable in terms of those duties which are claimed to exist by the doctor and his colleagues.   Necessarily, this precludes the possibility that duty could relate to other than professional perceptions, i.e. that there may be a general social duty to save life or not to kill which is independent of the nature of professionally received wisdom or practice.   Secondly, of course, ex hypothesi it fails to take account of the actual intention of the doctor, by inferring his intention from the fact that behaviour of this type is professionally acceptable.   Clearly, it is always difficult to interpret the intention behind a given act.   This will in most situations be inferred from other circumstances, for example the fact that the act was done, or the foreseeability of the consequences and so on. Equally, we may seek to impute blame where we see the act, or the person making the omission, as being self-interested in terms of the anticipated result. Thus, we may wish to impute moral blame to the parent who kills the child, or omits to feed it, on the grounds that his/her self-interest is served by the decease of the child, while we may regard other decision-makers as disinterested, and therefore perhaps more acceptable. In some ways, however, this may seem to allow a dangerous or harmful act or omission to avoid culpability even where the sole intention was that the baby should die, simply because it was part of normal, disinterested professional practice that such babies should be allowed to die. In other words, reference to standard practice can tell us nothing about the actual intention of the doctor. Intention may, however, be implied by the nature of the means adopted to bring about the result. Thus, where the behaviour resulting in death is an act rather than an omission, it may be simpler to impute intention.

While it may be that the concept of reasonable practice is of fundamental importance where what is being alleged is that the doctor was negligent,[17] there are less clear reasons for using it as a guideline in matters where the issue at stake is a general social liability through the device of the criminal law. Equally, the result of the judgments in the Arthur case would seem to be that the doctor's motivation is of fundamental importance, and that, although technically he may be held liable for an omission, this omission itself, even although it may seem culpable, will only be legally culpable where it differs from or is not supported by, reasonable or normal practice

It should be pointed out here that, in the event, Dr. Arthur was found not guilty of attempted murder both on the grounds of his intention and on the grounds that the regime of nursing care only did not in fact amount to an attempt to kill the baby who was in fact moribund. What is of interest therefore is not that he was not convicted, since the evidence presumably indicated that he was not legally guilty of any crime, but rather that the decision took major account of the professional description of the doctor's duties to his patients.

Thus, it is not merely the exigencies of time and place which lead us to see the decisions taken by doctors as decisions which are, by the nature of medicine, good decisions and therefore not susceptible of outside comment or criticism. Indeed, there were many who felt that, even although his behaviour was vindicated by the verdict, Dr. Arthur should never have been tried in the first place. This view reflects an attitude towards medicine and its practitioners rather than a moral or legal position. Essentially, the doctor is, as has been claimed, in no better a position to make decisions about life and death than anyone else.[18] But who should be the decision-makers then if the doctor is unqualified? Many would claim that the parents should take these decisions. This attitude reflects two things. First, a belief in the technical or legal competence of such decisions, and second adherence to the side-effects doctrine already discussed, i.e. that those most affected are those most competent to judge. Whether it is the doctor or the parents who are seen as the best decision-makers here, it is clear that it is pre-supposed that the strict application of the doctrine of the sanctity of life is precluded. Not only is this attitude susceptible of moral argument, it is also not a reflection of the state of the law. While parents do have limited rights over their children, they are for example not able to offer proxy consent to the use of their child for non-therapeutic experimentation.[19] In other words, they may agree to things which are for the benefit of their children but may not validly consent to things which harm them. So, unless we believe that babies are not harmed by being allowed to die or by being killed, then even if the parent has an emotional or practical interest in the fate of the baby he or she has no clear legal role in the matter. This is made quite clear in the case of Jehovah's Witnesses, whose religious beliefs may lead them to refuse to consent to the provision of a blood transfusion, but whose beliefs will be secondary to the expressed aim of the law to protect the vulnerable from this type of proxy overriding of what is in the interests of the child.

The acquittal of Dr. Arthur did nothing to affect the theoretical legal protection offered to children. What it did do was to say that this particular doctor had not killed or attempted to kill this particular child. In the case of babies, whether damaged or not, it would seem that while the moral situation remains confused,

72

the legal response does have the benefits of at least superficial clarity.

The Elderly or Terminally Ill.

Many of the arguments relating to babies also apply to those who are dying or are elderly and perhaps senile. The sanctity of life doctrine, in its modified double-effect version, may, however, be more applicable here. Where the patient is in pain, then by the application of double-effect, this may be relieved by pain-killers, even although a known consequence will be to hasten death.[20] Both this doctrine, and the general rules of law, depend on the nature of intention, and both would be likely to conclude that where the intention is not to kill, then no crime will have been committed. However, it is more difficult to justify killing the elderly on the moral grounds which would permit infanticide.[21] Clearly the elderly are not replaceable in the same way as babies, since they have a place in the community which is not readily replaced by the birth of another, for their death cannot readily be directly linked to the likely birth of another worthwhile life. Equally, there is no doubt that most of the elderly or terminally ill will have an interest in life, since they will have the conceptual ability to express a preference for life over death. We are, as has already been discussed elsewhere, not entitled, on at least one possible view, to override that preference even where we may feel it to be in their interests to do so.

Nor is there any doubt that the relative shortness of our prospective life is an irrelevant consideration to the moral or legal view of our right to life. The mere fact that the life-expectancy of the victim is limited does not justify killing. Thus, it is as much a crime to kill a person who is dying as it is to kill someone who may have had the prospect of thirty years of life. In other words, the condemnation of killing does not depend on the state of the victim, or even on whether or not he agrees to the killing, but on the intrinsic wrongness of killing.

There is, however, at least one of the doctrines applicable to children which might be considered to be important or relevant in the case of the terminally ill or elderly, namely the one which invokes the quality of life. The same responses, including the thin end of the wedge argument would, however, apply in this case. However, if concepts do form an essential part of desires then what are we to do with the comatose patient (elderly or not)? To some extent the answer to this will depend on whether or not we can accept two things. First that a pre-existing preference for life over death should remain extant until revoked. Second, that consciousness is an essential precondition of having desires. If we accept the former of these then killing or letting die may be morally culpable, while the latter would suggest that acts or omissions resulting in death could be justifiable in these cases.

However, consciousness is not always deemed to be essential to the protection of life. Equally, even in those cases where a person is taken to hospital comatose after voluntarily taking an overdose of drugs in an attempt at suicide, we do not respond as if this precludes the potential of a preference for life on recovery. Nor should the fact that recovery seems unlikely influence our moral stance, since this prediction is based on purely scientific prognoses which are of course fallible, and in any event make no pretence to offer us more than a technical explanation of medical condition.

It is in situations such as this, however, that the essential dishonesty of the acts/omissions doctrine becomes most clear. The purpose of differentiating between the two, the very reason for wanting to draw the distinction, is to excuse from moral blame in circumstances where a death is contemplated. Thus, the person who merely stands by and fails to treat pneumonia is less culpable than he who gives poison or a lethal injection. The act or omission, however, is equally overriding of our personal autonomy, since it takes no account of any pre-existing preference which we might have for life over death. Equally, it fails to take account of other factors. For example, we are assumed to have a preference of life over death even when we are not able, by reason of sleep, for example, to state or conceptualise that preference. Does this then make it possible to override an assumed desire simply because our condition is deemed to be irreversible?

This takes us back to the original point about our dependence on scientific information for our evaluation of moral or legal truths. The fact that we are told that a condition is irreversible on current scientific knowledge does not of course mean that it actually is. Indeed, the recent controversy about brain stem death centred on the fact that scientific prediction was an inaccurate and fallible basis on which to make decisions about life and death.

In the case of the adult patient, there is a further problem which may serve to influence our attitude in such cases. While the baby has no concept of death, and therefore cannot fear it, there is a genuine reason for using a variation of the thin end of the wedge argument in the case of those who will normally be predisposed to favour life over death, and that is that the fear of death in others will be exacerbated by the knowledge that in certain (unclear) situations we may seem to be candidates for death, perhaps merely by virtue of our being unable to express our opinion on the matter. This fear is a powerful argument since it relates not simply to the person whose future is under consideration but also to others. To adopt such an approach would be a diminution of our morality as a community, and would seriously affect the faith that we place in decision-makers, and cannot therefore be entirely excluded from our calculations.

In any event, if we are prepared to countenance the taking of such decisions, there is no clear answer to the question of who should be the decision-makers. Doctors are no better qualified than others to make such choices on behalf of others, since their training can tell them only the medical prognosis. Further, as we have seen, the element of self-interest which may form part of the parent's decision may make him or her a less than satisfactory decision-maker in such a fundamentally important area. The fact that the resolution of this problem is difficult, if not impossible, is perhaps a sufficiently cogent reason in itself to proscribe decision-making of this sort without reference to, or against the wishes of, the person under consideration.

Conclusion

Where then do these comments leave us? While we have seen that few moral doctrines actually support entirely the right of all of us to live, we have also seen that few of the arguments which offer criteria for deciding about death are entirely satisfactory. Indeed, we have seen that our dependence on a modified view of the sanctity of life may in some situations countenance a slow death, and perhaps a painful one, but would rule out the possibility of a quick and painless death, since the responsibility which we have for our acts is generally greater than that which we have for our omissions. Nor do the opposing views stand up to close scrutiny or give a consistently acceptable basis from which to make our selections and choices. It may be then that some groups in the community must be committed to a policy of saving all life which can be saved, the corollary being that we cannot kill life deliberately or deliberately leave to die.

However, merely to state this baldly as a type of commitment is also unsatisfactory, since it takes no account whatsoever of the consequences of this behaviour. If what we have to argue for is a type of sanctity of life doctrine, perhaps modified only by possibilities and by the principle of double-effect (insofar as this is generally acceptable) then what are the implications? Clearly, to save all life which is capable of being saved, while apparently a laudable aim, will have significant effects on all of us. Our natural aversion to the grossly deformed and the severely handicapped, and our (perhaps selfish) views about the humaneness and expense of keeping a senile elderly person alive when all purpose has gone from that life, may make us wish to modify that extreme position. In any event, our moral code is unlikely to be an absolute one since the commitment to being humane may serve to override a commitment to the absolute inviolability of all human life.

What is clear is that merely by permitting decisions about life and death to be taken by those whose role deals with such issues most often, i.e. the doctor, will not resolve the problem, but will merely involve us in yet more convoluted attempts to rationalise our behaviour in so doing. To pass the responsibility for such life or death decisions to one group of selected individuals is not to guarantee either that the problem will disappear, or that its resolution will satisfy that part of our moral intuition which demands fairness and justice.

Clearly, were we to hold all life to be of equal value, and therefore equally deserving of being saved, we should require to make major changes in our society. It is an inescapable fact that we do not strive to save all live, nor do our political and financial priorities as individuals or as a community make the saving of all life a priority. To hold to a clear and defensible position, we would have to rethink these priorities, and radically alter our attitudes to the type of life which we offer these persons or groups. Once the initial choice of life or death has fallen on the side of life, there can be no doubt that the morality of our decision is dependent to some extent on the nature of the provision which we then make for those who are not 'normal' or healthy. Making a humane decision initially, cannot defend us against the charge that our manner of dealing with the consequences is obscene and immoral.

NOTES

1. For further discussion, see chapters 1 - 3, supra.
2. See chapter 3, supra.
3. See chapter 1, supra.
4. See, for example, Buchanan, A., 'Medical Paternalism', (1978) 7 Philosophy and Public Affairs, 370.
5. For a fuller discussion of these arguments, see Glover, J., Causing Death and Saving Lives, Harmondsworth, Penguin Books, 1977.
6. op.cit., chapter 12.
7. op.cit., at p. 158.
8. op.cit., at p. 162.
9. For further discussion, see chapter 3, supra.
10. This is the position at common law in Scotland; in England and Wales it is covered by the Congenital Disabilities (Civil Liability) Act 1976.
11. R v. Adams [1957] Crim. L.R. 365, at p. 375.
12. Statement made to the 'Daily Telegraph' 15 February 1982; quoted in Havard, J.D.J., 'The Legal Threat to Medicine', Brit. Med. J., Vol. 284, 27 February 1982, 612-3.
13. Havard, loc.cit., at p. 612.
14. Re B [1981] 1 W.L.R. 1421.
15. See particularly 'The Times' 4, 5 November 1981.

16. This is not the first case where such considerations have been discussed. See, for example, R v. Bateman (1925) 19 Cr. App. Rep. 8.

17. For further discussion, see chapter 8, infra.

18. For further discussion, see chapter 10, infra.

19. For further discussion, see chapter 6, infra.

20. R v. Adams, supra cit.

21. For further discussion, see Glover, op.cit., chapters 13 and 14.

5 Consent

Fundamental to the technical lawfulness of all medical intervention is the requirement that the patient concerned must consent to whatever treatment the doctor decides is appropriate to the particular condition. Consent is required primarily as a device to ensure that no unlawful interference takes place with the person or personality of the individual. Traditionally it is deemed to be a means of protecting the right to self-determination which it is held all people have. In other words, rules about the provision of consent are a method of providing for the protection of the autonomy of the individual.

Such is the interest in ensuring that exploitation of the vulnerable does not take place that even those groups in the community who may be felt not to have rights to claim personal autonomy, for example babies and the unconscious, have been the subject of the development of rules whereby their interests may at least be expressed by proxy where they cannot be expressed personally. Clearly, although an extreme interpretation of the consent requirement might preclude any medical intervention in respect of these people, pragmatics dictate that there is some method whereby the benefits of medicine may equally be extended to them. Thus, a body of rules has been developed to define clearly those situations in which consent may be provided on behalf of these groups, and under what circumstances. Consent, then, has both a moral and a legal role to play, and underlies the whole of medical practice.

Further, there are other groups which have required the creation of rules governing consent by proxy, for example where the individual person is incapable of providing consent for other reasons, such as because of his mental condition or because of other legal incapacity, such as age. These rules permit intervention only where the consent of an authorised person has been gained on their behalf, again requiring that the intervention must be in the interests of the person concerned. To some extent, the problems surrounding the provision of consent in these groups are qualitatively different from those which are involved in the provision of consent in the more traditional and normal medical transaction. While in the former group the problems may centre on the authorisation of the person providing consent by proxy, and around questions of what may be deemed to amount to the best interests of the individual as well as the question of what amounts to a sufficient or 'informed' consent, the problems in the latter group are particularly concerned with the meaning of 'informed' consent.

'Informed' Consent

Informed consent is a term much used in contemporary legal discussion about consent in medical practice, and has even crept into some of the philosophical literature in this field. However, the term arose not as an attempt to provide a legal or moral doctrine or commitment, but rather as a means of narrowing and interpreting the conceptual definition of consent.[1] Its implications have been variously interpreted but there is growing acceptance of 'informed' as a prerequisite for the adequate provision of consent, at least for legal purposes. The use of this term, while its precise meaning is unclear, has emphasised the fact that consent, where properly provided, requires an element of receiving and understanding information. The major arguments in this area therefore centre on the extent of disclosure necessary to satisfy our conception of 'informed' consent by protecting the individual from the unwarranted assumption of authority, and to a lesser extent on the understanding of such information. Both are inextricably linked in the process of protecting the individual's autonomy, since 'To inform requires an efficient system of communication and to consent implies understanding.'[2]

The Arguments for Consent

The major arguments propounded in favour of the need for the provision of consent, are, as has already been indicated, largely derived from the perception which we have of the individual.   If we see the individual as a self-determining moral agent, then there are good reasons for demanding that no interference with that individual is permissible unless the person concerned actually agrees to that intervention.   This approach is to some extent predicated on an assumption that the information which is provided is given or expressed in such a way that the individual may understand at least the essentials of it.   Merely to 'inform' then, in the sense of giving information, is insufficient - a certain level of understanding must also be achieved before the possibility of a choice may actually be said to exist.   In this way, the imbalance of the medical transaction may be corrected.   As Pellegrino and Thomasma[3] point out:

> Value conflicts occur in a relationship of inequality inherent in the vulnerability of the patient...The assault of illness on the usual freedoms of the human being presents an immediate and present danger that the patient's values might be violated or that the physician may confuse technical and moral authority.   The patient's moral agency is at risk, and a special obligation of the act of [medical] profession is to protect that moral agency while treating the patient.[4]

While our moral approach to the individual tailors to a large extent our views on the need for consent to be provided, so too do our views of the aims and benefits of the proposed therapy.   While a certain amount of criticism has been levelled at the practice of medicine and the claims which are made about the value of therapy,[5] there is still a proportion of the community who would view decisions about the need for therapy, and the selection of therapy, as being matters for the doctor (as the involved professional with the appropriate expertise)[6].   Further it may be claimed that the patient has given this power to the doctor merely by voluntarily consulting him.   Clearly this will be a sufficient explanation of the role of the individual in medical transactions only if we adopt the extreme position that the doctor always knows best.

What then is it about our view of the individual which might lead us to insist on the provision of 'informed' or real consent? Morals, of course, is not a single unified doctrine with easily defined viewpoints and in this area it may be that the elements of morality which we can adduce to support our contention that consent is a necessary prerequisite of the legitimacy of medical intervention, will not ultimately be those which we would want to adopt either from a legal point of view or from the perspective of the pragmatic aims of medicine.

Morality may offer us a number of possible positions on the rights and interests of the individual which may lead us to different views of the nature and extent of the consent which should be provided. The most abstract and individualistic of these positions would be the 'absolute rights' of the individual type of argument which finds little sympathy in the worlds of law and medicine. While both law and medicine talk of using such an approach, as we have seen, the approach actually taken shows a less firm commitment than might at first appear. This approach assumes that the individual patient or prospective patient is a self-motivating moral agent with corresponding rights to complete self-determination and personal integrity. The logical implication of this view is that each patient in providing consent must do so not only free from duress and with the legal capacity to make rational decisions, but also only after consideration of (implying access to) all relevant facts which it is possible for him or her to know. Thus there must be disclosure of all factors which could conceivably be relevant to the choice to be made. This approach concentrates on the disclosure of information rather than on the use which is subsequently made of it. Thus, although requiring that information is given which allows for a rational choice be made, it does not demand that the individual makes use of these facts, since part of his freedom of choice must also include the freedom to ignore information and to take decisions spontaneously, or on other grounds.

One might wish to argue that such an approach loses some of its import if the patient need not take and use such information as a basis for choice since there is then little point in making disclosure of this type. However, if the reason for obtaining consent is simply to secure the right to self-determination, and this is not predicated, for instance, on the rationality of the individual, the use to which the information is put will not affect the nature and extent of the disclosure which is required. Thus it appears that only full disclosure of all known risks would satisfy a view of this type.

One modification of the 'absolute rights' approach is the thesis that the individual has a right to obtain information, but that this implies a corresponding duty to use that information in a rational way. This accords more readily with the views of those who hold the need for treatment, as medically defined, to be an overwhelming consideration. Further, it takes account of the wider possibility that the interests of the community are served by therapy. On this view, then, the individual rights which might be claimed are only a part of the full picture, since the wider community has legitimate interests in our subsequent behaviour. This argument does not exclude the right to personal autonomy, but serves to limit that right in situations where the individual is not the sole person affected by the choice. It can therefore be used to justify the compulsory notification and treatment of certain infectious diseases and may even be used to support the national policies which advise, for example, the vaccination of all children against whooping cough. While superficially appealing as an argument, this view has been criticised by some commentators who claim that its adoption entails that:

> The individual is subordinated to the greater 'needs' of the whole, preventive procedures become compulsory and the right of the patient to withhold consent to his own treatment vanishes as the doctor argues that he must submit to diagnosis, since society cannot afford the burden of curative procedures that would be even more expensive.[7]

It can be seen then that the major arguments which are used to support a rigorous application of the principle of 'informed' consent centre on the right of the individual to make personal and understanding choices about the manner in which his integrity may be affected. While other arguments may be used which shift the emphasis away from the rights of the individual, there are others which purport to accept the personal autonomy argument but serve to minimise its application.

One such argument is to the effect that, since the patient

presents himself for treatment then in the normal run of the mill medical transaction, his consent can be assumed from this fact alone. Thus, where the sane, adult person consults, for example, his general practitioner, he is impliedly consenting to whatever treatment the doctor may then decide to attempt. This argument does not of course actually totally exclude consideration of personal autonomy since it clearly only applies in those situations where the patient voluntarily makes the consultation, but it does reduce the right to autonomy to the decision to seek advice or treatment.[8] Individual self-determination is reflected only in the choice to seek advice or therapy, and not in the decision whether or not to take that advice or undergo that therapy.

To interpret the right to autonomy in this narrow sense is unsatisfactory, but this is often the line taken by doctors, and by others whose belief in the medical nature of decision-making is strong or absolute. It is, however, relatively easy to regard this as an acceptable type of view when we consider the nature of the legal requirements and the standard medical interaction. There is no legal, and no moral, requirement about the means by which consent can be legitimately expressed, i.e. it is not necessary for the patient to verbalise his consent to treatment. In large numbers of medical transactions, the patient indicates his consent to the proposed treatment merely by accepting the prescription and using the drugs. However, the fact that we may express our consent without resorting to formal procedures has no bearing on the nature of the consent itself. In particular it does not preclude the need for the explanation and disclosure which the 'rights of the individual' approach demands.

The Arguments against Consent

If the nature of consent is such that it requires both disclosure and understanding, then it is clear that there may be a strong body of opinion which would regard such requirements as inimical to the practice of medicine. There may be good practical reasons for claiming that to attempt to achieve such a high standard as full disclosure and understanding would be seriously to interfere with the medical enterprise. Such arguments, which have been formulated in a variety of ways, seem at first sight to give a relatively satisfactory explanation of the practice of not seeking consent.

First, it may be said that to require full disclosure is unreasonable, since the nature and extent of any individual doctor's knowledge may limit pragmatically the extent of disclosure which can be made. This argument is reinforced by the fact that the law does not require that doctors necessarily keep abreast of the medical literature even in their own specialism.[9] However, to claim that full disclosure would necessarily require a level of medical competence which goes well beyond that possessed by most doctors, is to misinterpret the nature of the disclosure which may be required. The assessment of what amounts to full disclosure will, in the tradition of the civil law, be based not on impossible standards but on the setting of a standard which is seen as reasonable in the circumstances. While this may reduce the nature of the information disclosed in some cases it may serve to raise it in others, and in any event this argument offers us no coherent reason to claim that the patient has no right to information: it serves merely to place a limitation on the amount of information which it is deemed necessary that a doctor has in order competently to practice his chosen profession. In any event, the fact that the doctor does not know all the medical information which it is possible to assimilate does not reduce the fact that 'It is essential that the patient be made to believe that he is an independent, worthy person entitled to the most clearly stated information possible.'[10]

Further, and to some extent following on from this, it may be argued that requiring full disclosure of information is unreasonable on the grounds that the patient will not understand the information presented so that no purpose will be served by providing it. This, of course, is paternalism at its most overt. Buchanan[11] convincingly illustrates the essential flaws in such a form of argument by claiming that since rules about disclosure are primarily designed for the safeguarding of the individual and not for the facilitation of the practice of medicine, the actual disclosure itself is what is fundamentally important. While understanding may be a separate and distinct problem, if an element of understanding is not a necessary concommitant of disclosure, the mere act of disclosure becomes valueless.[12] In any event, even if what is being sought is not an absolute position but rather the balancing of the rights of the individual and the interests of medicine, the patient's right to receive has a certain precedence over the doctor's duty to disclose. Indeed it may be on the right of the patient to receive information that the doctor's duty to disclose is based.

Moreover, while it is true that the patient will not necessarily understand, for instance, the intricacies of a surgical operation, it is not necessary for the protection of his autonomy that he does have such understanding. Indeed, it is also true of many doctors and nurses that, while they may be specialised in one part of medicine, they do not understand the technical intricacies of other parts. In any event, if this explanation is satisfactory it serves only to delimit the types of information which should be disclosed and not to preclude the need for any disclosure at all. The patient's rights of choice are protected not by his understanding, were this possible, of the technicalities of medical practice, but by his awareness and understanding of the invasiveness of the therapy proposed, its likely benefits and its likely risks.

The disclosure of risks and benefits, however, gives a further opportunity for medicine to show a paternalistic approach to disclosure. Thus it is often argued, and indeed has been accepted in some cases (notably by the Committee on Data Protection[13]) that certain information, and particularly that relating to risks, should not be disclosed to the patient since it might cause him distress. Not only does this assume that the patient will necessarily respond by being distressed, or that his distress will be sufficiently great to balance the minimising of his rights to self-determination which such withholding of information entails, but it is of course a prediction which goes beyond what we can reasonably call the expertise of the average doctor.

Further, it assumes that the distress of the patient is necessarily irrelevant to the calculation of whether or not to undertake the therapy. That is, if the patient is distressed by the risks entailed, it may be that he would rationally (or even irrationally, in medical terms at least) select on personal grounds not to take the treatment. In any case, arguments about distress and understanding of information may betray a lack of awareness of the fundamental importance of the medical act.   As has been said:

> The physician who is conscious of the special nature of
> his act of profession will not easily excuse himself from
> the obligation of disclosure on grounds that the patient
> cannot understand or will be harmed by the information.
> There is little if any evidence that such knowledge is
> deleterious...Indeed, in those rare instances in which the
> matter has been studied, informed patients show a lower
> anxiety and complication rate than the uninformed.[14]

Finally, the argument might be used that the patient need not
be told of all risks since some of them are small and that their
disclsoure might prevent him from undergoing the therapy on the basis
of a relatively small risk which might in any event never actually
occur.   It is certainly true that most medical procedures are so
well-rehearsed and so controlled that major risks are minimal.   There
may for example be a risk of death in every general anaesthetic, but
the controls of the procedure are such that the risk is very small.
However, whether or not the risks are major, bears no relationship to
the nature of the arguments about personal autonomy.

If the patient has rights to make choices, however medically
reasonable, then these rights must extend to the provision of
information on which to base these choices.   In any event it is clear
that the assessment of whether or not a risk is major or minor, and
whether or not it is worth taking, can in the nature of things be made
only by the individual concerned.   Only he knows, for example, the
importance which he would place on the relative likelihood of a risk
taking place, and this may depend on factors relating to the gravity
of his illness, its personal effects on him, the type of risk which
has a chance (however small) of occurring, and the impact which the
occurrence of that risk would have on his life.   We may choose to run
the risk of losing a limb, or losing our voice where the expected
benefit is the saving of our life or even the removing of severe pain,
but not if it is simply to relieve minimal distress.   Our assessment
of acceptable risks will also necessarily involve a decision about the
effects on our total life of the relevant risk.   It is essential that
the risk taken is one which is acceptable to the individual:

> That is to say, it must be as congruent as possible with
> his or her particular clinical context, values and sense
> of what is 'worthwhile' or 'good'.   What the physician

87

and the patient seek together is a judicious decision, one which optimizes as many benefits and minimizes as many risks as the situation will allow. The definition of risk is highly personal, and it turns on the patient's estimate of a danger 'worth' running.[15]

This aggregation of risks and benefits, while it may depend on medical information and may take account of medical advice, is nonetheless a personal decision based on our own reactions to the chances which we take.

The medical approach which supports these arguments is then an elitist rather than an individualistic one claiming, as it does, that one group, because of their technical competence in one area, has certain rights over another group who lack this knowledge, even although this competence may be the only difference. To accept this argument is to elevate one group to a powerful position over another simply on the basis of these acquired skills. However, it is also possible to present the same argument in pragmatic or utilitarian terms since it could be argued that the interests of the majority are best served by not having to cope with a large ill population. This expansion of the 'best interests' of the patients argument towards the best interests of the community and the efficient use of resources is much used by the law and medicine even although it is not always consistently applied (for example medicine does not always allocate resources to maximise benefits for the greatest number as in heart transplantation programmes and so on).[16]

Further, the arguments expressed in this way cannot and do not take account of the possibility that an increased level of disclosure would actually reflect well on the practice of medicine. It is not unreasonable to claim that, since it is generally agreed that trust is an essential basis of the doctor/patient relationship, an increased level of disclosure, leading to more sense of the partnership of the doctor and the patient in the medical transaction, might in fact benefit that relationship. It is also possible to claim that the raising of the standard of disclosure would bring to medicine a type of accountability at the consumer level which would be in the interests of the individual as well as of the community as a whole. Such arguments we should note further assume that treatment is a successful agent. They might be more convincing and more justifiable where there is more certainty of benefits.

Is it, then, inconsistent to accept on the one hand the general argument that the individual must be self-determining and on the other hand the view that medicine has a legitimate interest in withholding information in order to maximise health?   Although the positions seem at first sight to be poles apart, on closer examination the differences may sometimes be less fundamental.   Exceptions may be made to the extreme position of the individualist when competing interests arise, and in some cases, of course, self-motivation and personal intregrity may actually depend on cure, as in the case of mental patients.[17]   Quite apart from the problems arising when the person is legally incapax there are some patients whose rights to self-determination may depend on cure, for example those suffering from acute depressive illnesses may be unable to make use of the rights and benefits to which they are entitled, and which they may prefer to take advantage of.   In such cases, the view that therapy is a benefit may be seen as a contribution to safeguarding certain liberties and rights rather than as minimising the right of choice. Courts have therefore been prepared to excuse certain fairly substantial failures of disclosure where the anticipated benefits of therapy would facilitate the development of the individual.

This attitude, however, begs the question of the position of those who are in some way incapacitated, since the mere fact of incapacity cannot necessarily reflect on the rights of the person to claim freedom of choice.   By and large those who are, for example, mentally ill or under a certain age, are denied the use of certain rights which they would otherwise have.   However, this is a device designed, not specifically to deprive them of rights, but rather to ensure that they are not exploited in their vulnerable condition, although the effect might be the same.   Provision is, however, made for some decisions to be taken on their behalf by suitably authorised people.   Even although these decisions can be taken by proxy, there are necessarily limitations on them, the primary control being that the decision must be taken in their interests.   So, a parent can consent only to those procedures which are in the interests of the child, and may not technically agree to the use of their child in non-therapeutic experimentation.   And so, while the actual freedom of choice may be limited in this way, in view of the incapacity of the person, this arrangement enables the incapax to reap the beneficial

89

aspects of therapy.

The Legal Response

It is clear, then, that the moral approach which upholds the rights of the individual provides us with the most satisfactory protection for the individual who is necessarily an unequal partner in the medical enterprise, at least in terms of technical knowledge. The actual legal rights which may be extended to the individual will depend on which view (absolute rights or paternalism) or modification of these extreme positions, is adopted by the courts in their decision-making. The role the law has adopted is a median line between the rights of the individual and the exigencies of medical practice. The traditional legal device for the resolution of conflicts in this area has been to use the test already described as the usual one in the civil law, i.e. the test of reasonableness. Thus, the law has attempted to take decisions about whether or not the extent of the disclosure which was made in any set of circumstances was one which could be equated with reasonable or standard medical practice. This is the inevitable result of the intervention of the law, since it adopts a modification of the 'absolute rights' approach and of paternalism. The conclusion would logically be that absolute positions are unacceptable and that the amount of information which is required or wanted by any one patient may vary with the individual.

There are two ways in which this assessment of reasonableness may be made. One is the device of assessing what the reasonable patient would have done in any set of circumstances, and the other is to estimate what disclosure would have been made by the reasonable doctor. While there may be differences in the way in which these assessments are made there is one point of similarity, that is the implicit belief that therapy is more likely to be a good thing than a bad thing. The reasonable doctor is not expected to disclose information which would stop the patient from undergoing therapy,[18] and the reasonable patient is deemed in some cases to be he who undergoes therapy which is seen as a good thing, even where he becomes damaged as a result. Thus, the law may indulge in predictions about what the reasonable patient would consider to be relevant information, or the weight which the reasonable patient would give each piece of information. Thus in some cases, even although the patient has claimed that certain previously undisclosed information would have led to a refusal of consent, the law has chosen to assess this claim not on the basis of individualistic arguments but by the reasonableness test which depends either on a perceived consensus of rational behaviour, or on assumptions about rationality in decision-making.[19]

The assessment of what characterises the reasonable doctor is also one which gives rise to problems. Reasonableness will depend not just on the extent of disclosure, but also on the way in which disclosure is made. Thus, as we have already seen, mere provision of unintelligible information is unlikely to satisfy our moral claims, nor will it by and large satisfy the legal requirements. It is probably true that the doctor is not entitled deliberately to obfuscate the situation, and assuming that disclosure is made reasonably then the legal duty to disclose will have been fulfilled. Understanding, of course, is important in terms of the making of a rational choice but as we have seen making such a choice is not an essential part of the individual's claims to rights in these areas since they may, even having understood completely the information disclosed, nonetheless choose to make an apparently irrational choice. However, it is important that he has the information to make an 'informed' judgment even if he does not choose to do so. Thus, one possible view from a particular moral standpoint is that each individual has fundamental rights to receive information (whether or not he is capable of understanding it or acting rationally as a result of it) and this, therefore, places a corresponding duty on the doctor to make disclosure in order to allow for the greatest possible maximisation of self-determination.

However, not surprisingly, this viewpoint finds little support from medicine which tends to prefer a 'best interests' type of approach which places medical practitioners in a position of interpreting and sifting information and assessing what it is in the interests of the patients to know. Thus the duty to disclose, while widely accepted by doctors, takes on a new and paternalistic aspect. While this may be ethically or morally defensible, its results may sometimes be bizarre. It is entirely consistent for doctors to hold this position in line with their philosophical and professional commitment to healing or curing, even although it may in fact conflict with the best interests of the patient in the short or long term. Further, doctors may claim that, if our argument that information must be disclosed but need not be used is valid, then this is further justification for their failure to make disclosure of certain facts, since only a rational choice could be in the interests of the patient. This, again, is consistent with their philosophy which is dependent on ideas of preventing, treating or alleviating illness, but it does ignore the possible claim that there is a right to remain or become ill rather than accept treatment or prevent ill-health.

Viewed from this angle it is clear that the doctor's position is unusually extreme since, of course, we are all already in a position of having the right to become or at least not be explicitly prevented from becoming ill by deliberate choice through, for example, smoking, and drinking alcohol, as well as inadvertently or carelessly through bad eating habits and so on.

It may be, however, that the medical view is valid but only where it can be applied. Thus we cannot on an individual basis control pollution in the atmosphere nor single-handedly and deliberately ensure that only healthy food is eaten, but we can make rational choices one-to-one where we are confronted with individual patients with individual and curable illnesses. This 'best interests' approach crops up at all levels of society from our criminal justice systems to the compulsory wearing of seat belts and limitations on the sale and manufacture of, for example, harmful drugs. It is also widely used to justify many actions of doctors in, for example, participating in the destruction of severely damaged foetuses or allowing new-born babies to die.[20] However, if rights to such fundamentals as self-determination are to mean anything then they must operate individually.

The need or rationale for decision making of the type outlined is derivative from the classification made by the law of the type of legal action which is appropriate to the claim that consent has not been validly given. If the failure to obtain consent is seen as an infringement of the rights of the individual, then the appropriate legal action will be that of assault or trespass against the person. Where it is viewed as an aspect of the doctor's duties to the patient however, then the appropriate action to be raised will be one in negligence which reflects the professional practice of the doctor rather than the rights of the individual.

The response of the law has been to attempt to marry the interests of the patient and the interests of therapy. At least, this is the superficial picture presented by a brief glance at the rules as they are stated. Clearly, the law has become less and less prepared to act solely in the interests of the individual, and this is evidenced by the move away from the assault based action towards the action based on negligence. Obtaining consent then becomes merely yet another aspect of duty, and not a principle fundamental to our personal autonomy.[21]

The attempts which have been made in some cases to define what the reasonable patient would have done in any given circumstances have equally reflected on the autonomy of the individual, by categorising his behaviour in a general rather than a particular way. The reasonable patient, as the reasonable doctor, is presumed to have a natural bias in favour of therapy, and this interpretation tends to be made unless the risk which was not disclosed was a particularly substantial one. These approaches, depending as they do on the interest of therapy, are necessarily less protective of the view of personal autonomy which we have discussed. All forms of rationalisation, depending as they do on balancing the interests of one group and the interests of another, involve a dissipation of the more individually protective stance taken by those whose fundamental interest is the personal autonomy of the individual.

It is clear, then, that there are some difficulties in reconciling the overall desire to protect the rights of the individual to claim self-determination with the interests of medicine and its therapeutic aims. Superficially it would appear that the law takes a pragmatic approach, attempting to combine both aspects of the 'best interests' concept in order to reap the greatest benefits for the greatest number. This, of course, is often one of the practical results of the law although it may not be its primary aim. Rather the law may claim to support the individual qua individual rather than as part of a group. However in its attitude to the question of consent to medical treatment we can see that, as in other areas involving medical practice, the law gives priority to the general good of medical treatment rather than to the interests of the individual.

This is evident on two counts. First, in the limitation of the traditional use of the assault/battery/trespass action, and secondly in the corresponding use of concepts such as 'reasonable' doctor and 'reasonable' patient.

In allegations of lack of consent in respect of medical treatment the assault based action bears little precise relationship to the assault action in the criminal law which requires proof not just of the act but also of mens rea or the criminal intention necessary to make an act criminal. Consent is not therefore a defence to a criminal charge except where lack of consent is an essential constituent of the charge, for example in the case of rape.[22] On an assault action based in the civil law the essential element is the interference with the individual and the evidence that it was not consented to. It is this ability to render lawful an action which would otherwise be unlawful which primarily differentiates civil assault from criminal assault. In criminal cases the fact that the victim consents to, for example a serious assault will not render the act lawful, whereas in medical practice what might otherwise be a very dangerous act, for example major surgery, can be rendered lawful by the provision of consent by the patient. Where such consent is obtained no legal right of action will exist. But it is the nature of this consent which causes primary problems.

This is so because the provision of consent requires not just the legal capacity to offer consent, which by in large can be fairly readily assessed (surrogate consent may be appropriate in the best interests of the incapax) but also an element of disclosure which makes choice in the circumstances a real possibility. To some extent courts have limited the ability to assess what is real consent by the use of the concept of 'informed consent'. The implications of the word 'informed' may make allowance for the use of arguments such as 'only a brain surgeon could understand brain surgery', thus disguising a paternalistic attitude and failing to take account of the primary function of the requirement that consent must be given. While this is primarily an American concept, it is nonetheless creeping into British cases, and its continued use implies also that there are standards against which the behaviour of a given doctor in respect of

the given patient can be tested. The major benefit of using terms
such as 'informed' in these areas is, as we have seen, the implication
that understanding has also been achieved, but this implication exists
even where we limit our terminology to that of real rather than
informed consent.

Thus, the right of action which may stem from the failure to
obtain sufficient consent exists primarily to protect the
inviolability of the individual and to safeguard his right to make
choices. In this way it may protect the integrity of the individual
against the unwarranted assumption of authority by someone else, no
matter the motivation of the intervention or its potential benefits.
The extent to which consent can be real is, of course, problematic
given that the technical arguments produced by medicine are not
entirely irrelevant. And it is particularly problematic if we
assume, as we must, that consent does imply an element of
understanding whether or not the choice made in the long run is
rational or irrational. At the simplest level the 'realness' of
consent may be related to the personal characteristics of the patient
or prospective patient, for example as in the case of the incapax.
The rationale for excluding the incapax from the provision of consent
is largely that he cannot be certain to make choices which are in his
own interest, which would not substantially differentiate him from the
rest of the community on one possible view. However, the incapax
must also be protected from exploitation, and it is this consideration
which makes it imperative that choices are made by proxy. This does
not however reduce the level of disclosure which should be made to the
person authorised to make the choice, nor does it tailor his decision,
beyond the fact that his perception of his choice must be in the best
interests of the incapax.

Assault vs. Negligence

The use of the assault action where it is alleged that consent was not
properly or fully obtained provides support for the claim that the
central feature of the action is the intervention in the integrity of
another individual. It does not matter whether or not measurable
medical harm resulted from the intervention, nor does it matter what

the patient's view would have been had disclosure been made fully. This type of action places fundamental emphasis on the patient and the patient's right to receive information, rather than on the doctor's duty to provide information, although the latter is predicated on the former. A premium is therefore placed on the freedom to make a choice, whatever that choice may be, and potentially this type of action demands a higher standard of disclosure by doctors than does the negligence based action. For some time the assault based action was the primary means of seeking redress in the courts. However, the trend now seems to be that this is considered an inappropriate basis on which to sue in medical practice.

The current trend away from the use of the assault action in civil cases involving medical intervention, has led to the replacement of this action by the use of the negligence action. As has been seen, this parallels the view now apparently adopted that the provision of consent is a reflection of the duties of the doctor rather than of the rights of the individual, and is confirmed by the recent case of Chatterton v. Gerson and Another,[23] in which the court made it clear that the appropriate action where lack of consent is alleged is an action in negligence.

There are several possible reasons for this shift of emphasis. First, it may be that there is a general distaste for the implications, on a non-technical basis, of the terminology of assault being applied to medical practice. It is not unlikely that many may feel that this type of action is inappropriate when dealing with professionals whose aim and motivation is to heal, and whose curing techniques will almost invariably mean intervention at a physical level. However it is intention rather than the motivation which is generally of importance to the law, and to treat without consent must be seen as an assault on the physical integrity of the individual patient.

Secondly, there are more technical difficulties in the use of the assault based action since it is unclear whether or not the use of drugs could amount technically to an assault as traditionally conceived. Some definitions of assault provide a sufficiently wide scope to include pharmaceutical intervention with the body's metabolism, whereas other more traditional definitions of assault may seem to preclude what is probably medicine's most common form of treatment.

For the patient, however, there are clear implications of this change of base. To hold that obtaining consent is part of a doctor's duty to his patients results in a corresponding shift of interest away from the right of the individual to receive information, and by implication, to make choices. However, logically the right of the patient and the duties of the doctor are not mutually exclusive, since the doctor may have a duty which is based on the individual's right of self-determination, and that duty will therefore only be meaningful where he actually attempts to protect such a right. From the doctor's point of view the necessity of obtaining consent may be viewed as a means of safeguarding against the risks of subsequent legal action, but this does not in se make it a professional duty. If it is a duty, then it is a general rather than a purely professional one, arising rather from the patient's right to be informed rather than solely from professionally wise or prudent practice.

Thus the essential feature even of the negligence type of action should logically remain the right of the patient upon which the doctor's professional duty hinges. This duty to inform can be differentiated from other duties which doctors may have in respect of their patients, such as a duty to offer treatment or a duty not to abuse the patient. It follows then that the move to the negligence action need not necessarily demand that the interests of patients are given second place to the duty of the doctor to treat, to his professional status, or to a generalised assessment of what a doctor's duties actually amount to.

It has already been claimed that the shift to the negligence action, however, has in practice precluded the ability of the courts to make decisions on individual cases. Rather, by adopting this form of assessment, they have chosen to employ notions such as reasonableness in interpreting a doctor's duty to a patient. This is very much in line with other decisions which are taken within the negligence framework, but essentially the nature of 'consent' decisions differs in quality from these decisions. While it may be rational to judge a doctor's behaviour by that of his colleagues where the test is being applied to the particular skills of medicine,[24] it is less obvious that this is an adequate basis for decision-making where what is being considered is not his technical expertise, but his essentially uninformed decision as to which information will be harmful to a patient, or which information may deter a patient from treatment. It is this possible view of the best interest of the patient which causes major conflict. The lack of consent is primarily a problem for the patient, since the doctor may perform an immaculate job and yet still restrict the rights of his patient by not providing him with the opportunity of choice. To see failure to obtain consent solely as a failure in professional duties is surely to fail to take the major point about rights of individual determination and integrity.

However, there is another more pragmatically problematic result of the shift from the assault to the negligence action, which reflects the ideological conflicts already outlined and has serious implications for the patient attempting to sue. First, there is the fact that measurable harm must have resulted from the doctor's behaviour where the action is based in negligence, which automatically rules out a successful action where the intervention was of benefit to the patient in medical terms. Secondly, and more insidiously, the negligence action depends on notions such as standard practice and reasonableness which automatically shift the emphasis from the individual doctor or patient to the more abstract considerations of general practice. This may also allow the interests of medical science and 'cure' to override the expressed interests of the individual. Thus decisions in cases such as Hatcher v. Black[25] have allowed the doctor to lie to his patient, or not to make disclosure of essential facts, since the best interests of the patient are thought to be served by the intervention of medicine.

Conclusion

The essential problem then in all discussions about consent is the element of disclosure, and also what decisions can properly be called 'medical'. Our views about disclosure of information and about the nature of technical decisions will serve to influence or predict the type of legal rights which we will extend to the individual. An individualistic approach might in its extreme form dictate that all relevant information should be disclosed, even where the risk is minimal as opposed to special, so that the patient may reach his decision in the light of his own personal circumstances. Doctors may, however, claim that the best interests of the patient are not served by full disclosure, but rather by non-disclosure of certain particularly slight risks even although these risks may be particularly harmful to the patient should they occur. Medicine may take an essentially pragmatic approach in saying that where the risk is minimal the interests of the individual (and perhaps even of the majority) are best served by non-disclosure of such risk. This, however, would conflict with the idea that each individual should take a choice in the light of the fullest possible information.

The courts seem to have adopted a very wide view of what can properly be called 'medical' decisions. This ignores the personal nature of decision-making and reduces its non-technical constituent, thereby limiting the freedom of choice of the individual. One possible alternative view is to see decision-making as more subtle and more complex, and to accept that:

> ...doctors must be the arbiters of those questions which are technical. Thereafter, the issue is an ethical one, even including the question of how far such technical information is to be deemed relevant to the conclusion to be reached.[26]

The participation of the patient in the ethical content of medicine is unlikely to be so readily disputed as is his right to technical information.

It has been left to the law to attempt a balance between these two apparently conflicting interests in respect of consent and disclosure, and it has tried to do this as we have seen by conceptualising the problem in terms of a doctor's duty rather than in terms of a patient's right and by interpreting the best interests approach with the potential benefits of therapy very much in mind. This it does primarily by using the device of the negligence action rather than the assault based action. The result of this may be to protect the doctor rather than the patient by allowing a freedom of medical intervention which at least in the short term our moral views might not countenance.

What amounts to the best interest of the patient may then turn out to be a primary source of disagreement between the various disciplines. It would appear that both medicine and the law regard the best interests of the patient as being served by receiving treatment and by avoiding the distress which might be caused by informing him of all of the risks which might occur in the course of any given treatment. The goals of the individualistic moral approach, however, may be served precisely by requiring that such information is disclosed, and its claim may be that the best interests of the patient relate more to other general considerations than merely to his medical condition. In any event it is claimed that there is no evidence that disclosure of risks will cause upset to patients.[27] Of course, in the event that most patients would nonetheless even in full knowledge of the risks accept treatment, then the interests of his physical well-being could also be served by this approach. Certainly there is no evidence that a substantial or significant number of patients would in fact refuse treatment even if they knew all the risks (particularly where they knew the percentage likelihood of the risks taking place), or at least there is no evidence that a rational balancing of risks will not take place.

While a restriction on disclosure might be justified where the level of non-participation reaches a level at which others are put at risk, it is not clear that it is sufficiently justified where the amount of risk to others is minimal, or even marginally increased. Equally, the number of patients likely to become ill and severely distressed as a result of knowing all the risks is again likely to be small. In the long run therefore the interests of the individual (and perhaps of the community) may best be served by disclosure of information, and there can be no doubt that the status of the individual as a self-motivating agent is significantly enhanced by allowing him freedom of choice.

NOTES

1. For discussion, see for example, Skegg, P.D.G., '"Informed Consent" to Medical Procedures' 15 Med. Sci. & Law 124 (1975).
2. Ajayi, O.O., 'Taboos and Clinical Research in West Africa' 6 J. Medical Ethics (1980) 61.

3. Pellegrino, E., and Thomasma, D., A Philosophical Basis of Medical Practice, O.U.P., 1981.

4. ibid., at p. 212.

5. See, for example, Illich, I., Limits to Medicine. Medical Nemesis: The Expropriation of Health, Harmondsworth, Penguin Books, 1977 edition; Kennedy, I., The Unmasking of Medicine, London, George Allen & Unwin, 1981.

6. For further discussion, see chapter 10, infra.

7. Illich, op.cit., at p. 104.

8. For further discussion, see McLean, S.A.M., and McKay, A.J., 'Consent in Medical Practice' in McLean, S.A.M., (ed), Legal Issues in Medicine, Aldershot, Gower Publishing Co., 1981, 96.

9. Crawford v. Board of Governors, Charing Cross Hospital [1953] T.L.R. 1.

10. Bernarde, M., and Mayerson, E.W., 'Patient and Physician Negotiation' J. American Med. Association, Vol. 239, No. 4, (1978) 1413.

11. Buchanan, A., 'Medical Paternalism' (1978) 7 Philosophy and Public Affairs 370.

12. For further discussion, see Robertson, G., 'Informed Consent to Medical Treatment' 97 L.Q.R. 102 (1981).

13. Cmnd. 7341/1978.

14. Pellegrino and Thomasma, op.cit., at p. 214.

15. ibid., at p. 124.

16. For further discussion, see infra chapter 10.

17. Indeed, this view was particularly influential in the case of Bolam v. Friern Hospital Management Committee [1957] 2 All E.R. 118.

18. ibid.

19. See, for example, the American case of Canterbury v. Spence 464F 2d 608 (1957); see also the British case of Hatcher v. Black 'The Times' 2 July 1954.

20. See chapters 1-4, supra.

21. See, for example, the case of Chatterton v. Gerson & Anor. [1981] 1 All E.R. 257, where it was made clear that the obtaining of consent was fundamentally a part of the doctor's duties to his patient, and that the appropriate action therefore in the event of a failure to obtain informed consent

was one in negligence.

22. For consideration of the role of consent in the criminal law, see Gordon, G.H., _The Criminal Law of Scotland_, (2nd Ed.), Edinburgh, W. Green & Son Ltd., 1978; Williams, G., _Textbook of Criminal Law_, London, Stevens & Sons, 1978.

23. supra cit.

24. For further discussion, see chapter 8, infra.

25. supra cit.

26. Kennedy, op.cit., at p. 150.

27. Pellegrino and Thomasma, op.cit., at p. 214.

6 Experimentation

It is often claimed that advances in medicine, both technologically and practically in terms of novel therapy, are as essential to the welfare of mankind as they are to the advancement of medical understanding and so-called medical science. For the purpose of this discussion, the use of the term experimentation will be taken to include both technological and pharmaceutical advances and the use of new methods of treatment. Thus, we must consider not only the more controversial points relating to the use of human subjects in the testing of new drugs and therapies, but also those which involve the wider exercise of clinical judgment. This discussion will concentrate on overtly new therapies and techniques, which pose their own special problems, while recognising that all medicine is a form of experimentation, since 'Each treatment is one more repetition of an experiment with a statistically known probability of success'.[1]

Experimentation in medicine is widespread, and takes place at all levels. Quite apart form the fact that well known and well used therapies may have different and sometimes unexpected results in any given case, medicine requires to practise on human subjects in order to achieve two different aims. At one level, experiments may be necessary to test the safety of new products. Such experimentation will take place on a limited basis, and its risks may be unforeseeable. On the other hand, experimentation may be necessary when old therapies are used in the treatment of different complaints or where innovations in therapy take place as an essential aspect of patient care or in an effort to improve old practice. This type of experiment is more common, and forms a part of the doctor's clinical freedom.

Although there is considerable international concern about, and an element of international control of, human experimentation, the ambits of such concern are limited, and the terminology used, while providing a theoretical basis for human experimentation, does little to elucidate some of the problems arising from the use of human subjects in this way. The concern of international agreements, such as the Declaration of Helsinki, was primarily to demonstrate the international community's distaste for the atrocities committed by the Nazi doctors in the course of the Second World War. In so doing, these agreements provided a re-statement of the aims of medicine and supplemented the doctor's ethical commitments as expressed in the Hippocratic Oath.[2]

Their main concern was to provide a framework for human experimentation which would reinforce medicine's humanitarian philosophy, and at the same time to delimit the nature of experimentation. It was recognised, and again this was the result of the types of experiments whose control was felt to be necessary, that experimentation could be carried out for different reasons. The codes therefore differentiate between therapeutic experimentation (in the interests of the patient) and non-therapeutic experimentation (in the interests of science or future patients), reinforcing in both cases the human dignity of the research subject. Further, it is made clear that research on human subjects should be carried out only with the freely obtained acquiescence of the research subject, in the legitimate interests of knowledge or patient care (with the latter predominating), and on the basis of sound scientific hypotheses tested in the laboratory and on animals.[3]

It is noteworthy that the tacit assumption behind such codes is that experimentation, either therapeutic or not, will and should continue, evidencing that both the international community and medicine itself see a need for such experiments as a contribution to the development of patient care and the wider interests of medical 'science'. This commitment is based on the crucial assumption that medical advances are necessary in order to improve either the lot of the individual or the lot of the community, either currently or in the future. It is assumed that medical science must develop because change and novelty in this sphere are necessarily good things leading to positive results in terms of patient care. The 'science' of medicine is held to require the acquisition of new knowledge in order to benefit communities in the future, so that, for instance, although the information gleaned from experiments may be of little apparent use given the current state of the patient or the current state of knowledge, nonetheless its acquisition is of major importance to the future well-being of society.

While few would argue that medicine should be prohibited from developing, and even fewer would wish to see medicine unthinkingly criticised, an absolute commitment to 'advance' contains certain basic flaws. The most notable of these is the belief that every acquisition of medical knowledge and every technical innovation leads to improved health care. In fact, much research is repetitive and aimed less at patient care than at the exploration of scientific hypotheses or at the profitability of the pharmaceutical industry. For example, companies may seek to find an alternative drug to one, marketed by another company, which has been shown to be highly profitable. A full commitment to medical progress on such a view ensures the likely continuation of commercially motivated research on human beings. Further, the nature of much research, and indeed of much medical practice, is such that the amount of information to which the subject, the community or its representatives have access may be limited, either because of its technological sophistication or because much research is carried out behind closed doors. That is, the argument often used by medicine that the community or the patient will not understand the complications of advanced medical thinking or technology, may serve to reduce the flow of information between medicine and the community. Further, much early research is carried out at levels over which the community has no control since it is unlikely even to be aware that the research is going on. This not only reduces the accountability of researchers but may cast doubt on the clinical value of their work.

Our natural desire for medical advancement must therefore be tailored by our concern for the human subject, either ill or healthy. Indeed, one possible measure of medical advance might be a diminution of the risks to which patients and subjects are exposed by means of a rational reduction in the number and scope of experiments. Equally, our assessment of the value of experimentation as a scientific method, might be different if we view medicine more as an art requiring personalised skills and taking account of individual concerns and intersts, rather than as a science consisting purely or primarily of empirical generalisations which can be mechanically and routinely deployed.

It has, for example, been claimed that:

> idolatry of science overlooks the fact that research conducted as if medicine were an ordinary science, diagnosis conducted as if patients were scientific cases and not autonomous persons, and therapy conducted by hygienic engineers are the three approaches which coalesce into the present endemic health denial.[4]

Given medicine's patchy track record in the solving of major disease problems, it is certainly true that serious consideration must be given to research work which is based on imponderable factors and seeks intangible results. As has been said:

> a philosophy of medicine is needed to help clarify medicine's goals in relationship to those of a technological civilisation. Medicine suffers from an abundance of means and a poverty of ends.[5]

Given that there is at least a prima facie case for controlling human experimentation, in the light of the uncertainty of its aims and the very real risks to which it may expose its subjects, it is immediately clear that the device of international agreements and commitments can provide only the theoretical framework which may assist medicine in its search for a philosophical basis for overall assessment of its aims and practices. At a more practical level, however, it cannot achieve rational control of experiments. This is so not simply because of the lack of sanctions which can be applied in the event of breach of any such agreements, but also because they are stated in a general rather than a specific way. What such agreements can do, and have done, is to focus attention on the need to protect the integrity of the research subject, and to place the aspirations of medical advancement in their proper perspective. International codes therefore amount more to a theoretical framework for human experimentation than a complete basis for actual control.

Experimentation with New Products

In the development of new medical products, there must come a stage at which the value of a new product or technique can only be assessed by the use of human subjects as experimental subjects. It is at this stage that we can see the difference most clearly between the practice of medicine and true scientific disciplines. It has been said that 'Scientific method provides for experiments conducted on models. Medicine, however, experiments not on models but on the subjects themselves.'[6] However, since there would be limited value in any pharmaceutical product which had been tested only on animals, then it is clear that such experiments will continue to be necessary to the extent that drugs continue to be developed. Thus, it is clear that '....human medical experimentation must continue, or progress in drug treatment will cease',[7] and equally clear that this may involve a substantial commitment to human experimentation.

A certain amount of more obviously scientific investigation can, of course, be carried out in advance of the stage at which the drug requires to be tested on a human subject. However neither animal nor laboratory testing can predict with sufficient precision the effect of new drugs on the human metabolism. Moreover, controlled clinical trials do not necessarily guarantee the ultimate safety of a product, but merely predict the likely short-term outcome of a certain level of the drug in question. Tests, even on human subjects, have still left doubts about the safety of, for example, Debendox, which is a drug often prescribed during pregnancy and which some claim may have deleterious effects on the developing foetus.[8] However, the prescription and use of drugs is a very common example of the medical transaction and drug therapy has been most beneficial in the control and treatment of a number of diseases. Thus, from the point of view of patient care some human experimentation is necessary particularly where there is no corresponding drug already available. It can still, however, be strongly argued that the type of research work involved should be tailored more to the interests of the patient, or to the majority of present and prospective patients. Were this to be the major aim of the pharmaceutical industry then its interest in profit-making would necessarily be secondary to the welfare of the community or the individual. Equally, the pressures on doctors to participate in clinical trials would be reduced.

At present the doctor may feel that his career prospects are as much bound up in his ability as a 'scientist' as in his skills as a healer. This view is encouraged at some levels since, as Kennedy says,[9] the individual doctor's reliance on change and technology serves

> as both validation and vindication of his training and of his image of himself as really the scientist, problem solver and curer. It is this same mentality which fuels the search for so-called wonder drugs.[10]

There are therefore considerations in respect of the production and use of new pharmaceutical products which go beyond the bounds of medical care. The pharmaceutical industry is now responsible for much of the research work which takes place, and therefore has some considerable control over the types of products for which experimental programmes will be deemed necessary. To this extent experimentation on human subjects may be the result of the predominance of the marketing interests of these companies, whose profit margins have shown them to have a fine business sense and a considerable control over the prescribing habits of doctors. Thus the need for certain types of human experimentation is the result of the interests of drug companies in producing new products which will be both useful and profitable. There is no doubt that in the world of the pharmaceutical companies '...it is "mission-orientated" research that dominates',[11] and thus certain types of ailment will not necessarily receive the attention of the industry. Equally, the interests of the drug companies may also show a direct correlation with the prescribing practices of doctors. For example, a perceived substantial market for tranquillisers in the event of their frequent prescription, may result in considerable investment in research in this particular area.

International agreeements, not surprisingly, lay no particular stress on the question of profitability, in part because they originated at a time when there was less research of this type. The pharmaceutical industry has, however, grown considerably since these agreements were reached. Nonetheless, the general commitments of the codes apply equally to drug experiments as they do to other forms of experiment which may seem to be more overtly dangerous. If the acceptability of experimentation is related to its potential or actual benefits for mankind or the individual as these codes would seem to suggest, there must not only be a reasonable expectation of benefit but the welfare of the subject must be protected by ensuring that unneccesary research is not carried out.

One fundamental consideration in any research programme should therefore be this expectation of improvement. Change need not equate with good, although obviously it may lead to it. Consideration of the likelihood of benefit is of course difficult at the early stages of production, but an historical awareness might serve to contribute something to our assessment of changes. It remains the subject of debate whether or not there is any evidence that advances in technological medicine can be shown to have produced substantial benefits. This assumption is discussed in detail elsewhere[12] but it is worth noting at this point that many commentators contend that most real improvements in man's health relate to factors which seem to bear little or no overt relationship to the intervention of medicine. Thus, many diseases have been reduced or obviated by the increased control of sanitation, water purification and so on, while many of the illnesses which are of an infectious nature have shown patterns of behaviour which seem to relate to unknown factors rather than to advances or changes in medical practice or to the availability of drugs. Illich,[13] for example, sceptically claims that 'Awe-inspiring medical technology has combined with egalitarian rhetoric to create the impression that contemporary medicine is highly effective.'[14] His view is that 'The study of the evolution of disease patterns provides evidence that during the last century doctors have affected epidemics no more profoundly than did priests during earlier times.'[15]

The role of pharmaceutical development, even although open to some criticism, has however been central to such advances and improvements as have been made. It is perhaps paradoxical that it has also been one fraught with disaster, as the case of thalidomide illustrates.[16] Further, an increased awareness of the hazards of new drugs has resulted in a strict regulation of their marketing and production which has in turn led to an increase in the use of human subjects for experimental purposes, on the grounds that limited tests may highlight major defects or dangers before the general public become exposed to them. We should, however, consider the pressures of the pharmaceutical industry most carefully not only because of the dangers outlined above, but also because the harmful effects of drugs may take some time to become evident. Even human trials cannot generally be undertaken over a sufficient length of time to rule out all of the possible dangers, either to the individual patient or subject or to future generations. In these circumstances it cannot be taken as self evident that experimental development of new drugs is necessarily a boon to humanity. As has been said:

> Without the reasonable restraints imposed by philosophical critiques, medicine and its practitioners may unintentionally convert scientific and medical method into a muddled philosophy of human life.[17]

The Use of New or Alternative Techniques

The use of experimental techniques is perhaps less open to abuse and more justifiable in some ways than is the development of new drugs. Certainly, the use of new or alternative therapies, while containing an element of scientific interest, is primarily focused on the potential benefit to a given patient. Where accepted and routine therapies have failed, then the doctor may feel himself to be under an ethical and a professional duty to apply his scientific and healing skills to the problem. This may involve the use of established therapies in a new way, or the use or development of a new therapy, in other words it will involve a deviation from normal practice.

Such deviation is generally seen as a constituent of clinical judgment. The doctor is presumed to be free from pressures relating to the means by which he practises his skills. This is true to the extent that the doctor's behaviour offends in no other way against legal rules. Thus, although he may claim to have and to exercise a certain clinical freedom, this is bound up with notions of good faith and scientific credibility, to mean that the doctor must ensure that his choice of therapy is reasonable in any given case. The law would not therefore protect the doctor who practises overtly wrong (in the sense of scientifically inaccurate or inappropriate) therapy.

Doctors are bound by the common law in these cases, and in particular by the rules concerning negligence.[18] While courts have been persuaded of the benefits of advances, it is also clear that they wish to retain an element of control over the extent to which clinical judgment may be exercised, and particularly where the patient is damaged as a result of the intervention. The rule laid down in the case of Hunter v. Hanley[19] is most commonly used as the standard against which behaviour will be judged. Broadly the rule states that where it is alleged that a doctor was negligent in that he deviated from normal practice, there require to be proved three things. First, that there was a usual practice; secondly, that the doctor deviated from that practice; and thirdly (and most importantly) that the deviation was such that no doctor, acting with due skill and care would have carried out. Proof of the last and most fundamental of these three requirements will be, as in all cases of negligence, particularly dependent on the evidence of other doctors. While this may raise some problems, it also provides the potential for a certain scientific validity in the decision reached.

While some cases have arisen which have involved clear breaches of this general rule, the majority of experiments are a more subtle form of choice and innovation, which makes their external assessement less straightforward. The need to achieve a balance between protecting the use of clinical judgment and holding medicine and its practitioners to be accountable, makes decision-making in this area particularly problematic. One immediate problem is the difficulty of obtaining information about the practice of medicine, which makes the likelihood of challenge more remote. Although certain provision is made for the obtaining of information where legal action is under contemplation,[20] in the general medical transaction the patient is unlikely to know whether or not the therapy used was conventional or innovative. Secondly, the perceived need to allow freedom of choice, within certain limits, is undoubtedly essential to the good and beneficial practice of medicine.

The doctor then is only protected at law insofar as he does not unreasonably deviate from the standard practice accepted by reputable colleagues of the same level of competence. That is, in his involvement in immediate patient care he will be expected to live up to his commitment to do his best for his patient according to the professional standards of the time. The prospect of professional advancement, or the interests of scientific curiosity must be subordinate to the welfare of the particular patient. The doctor's professional commitment involves the use of tried and tested methods where they are likely to succeed, but it may also involve the application of original or novel therapy where such techniques have been unsuccessful. The law recognises this, but the dangers of unreasonable or unprofessional experimentation with untried techniques makes the control of such methods imperative.

How do we Control Experiments?

Doctors have a monopoly on health related matters in contemporary society. This allows them 'the exclusive right to determine what constitutes sickness, who is or might become sick, and what shall be done to such people',[21] which reinforces the claim that 'Those who develop and apply technology must be held accountable to all of us'.[22] Control over experimental programmes is a particularly crucial part of that accountability.

While it may be unusual to resort to the device of international law as a means of controlling professional practice, there can be little doubt that the internationally agreed codes of ethics are valuable as a clear statement of the aims and limitations which should be borne in mind by all those involved in innovation in medicine. However, at best they are fundamentally inefficient as a direct method of control, since they are backed by few sanctions in the event of breach and are far removed from the normal forum of medicine. Thus, contemporary medical practice continues to provide examples of experimentation which is either unnecessary or distasteful or both.[23] Checks at national level have therefore also been introduced to scrutinise and control experimentation, to ensure accountability and in particular to ensure that the 'engineer scientist model' is not 'reinforced at the expense of the model of the caring partner'.[24]

Our means of control are, however, necessarily limited, particularly since the confidential nature of most medical transactions is carefully guarded by the doctor, but also because of the rather insufficient interpretation of the rules about disclosure in consent.[25] Further, our controls are largely medicine dominated, relying heavily on the evidence and opinions of the colleagues of the researchers. This means that such controls as do exist may serve to reflect a purely, or substantially, medical view of the aims and morality of experiments with little weight attached to the competing claims of community based morality or perceptions.

In the United Kingdom, several layers of control and scrutiny have been developed in an attempt to control and monitor experimentation. While it has been assumed that the powers of the common law serve efficiently to control the potential abuse of clinical freedom, there has been a perceived need to introduce further controls in respect of new pharmaceutical products. In the United Kingdom, the central body controlling the marketing of new pharmaceutical products is the Committee on Safety of Medicines, which is part of the Medicines Commission.[26] This organisation seeks to ensure that no new pharmaceutical product will be marketed before its scientific hypotheses have been tested in the laboratory and on animals. Limited human trials under close supervision may then be authorised. This control reemphasises the need to protect at all times the welfare of the patient, so that experiments should cease at the point at which it seems likely that damage is occurring to the patient or group involved. Local medical bodies have also reinforced the integrity of the individual by reminding the doctor of the power relationship into which he enters with his patients, stressing the need to ensure that free consent is actually given.[27]

On a recommendation of the Medical Research Council, a further layer of scrutiny was developed by means of the institution of Research Ethical Committees in all hospitals where research is being carried out.[28] Nonetheless, it has been claimed that the way in which these committees have interpreted their function has often been uncertain, both in terms of the extent of lay representation on them and also in respect of their decision making.[29] The requirement for lay representation was seen as of crucial importance when these committees were instituted, in recognition of the fact that the aims of a developing 'science' and the interests of the community might not necessarily coincide in all cases. One further problem is of course that the nature of the decision structure is such that it necessarily precludes at present actual scrutiny of those sorts of human experiments which are likely to be more common, i.e. the choice between established therapies and the use of innovative ones.

113

Do We Need Controls?

It may be felt, however, that there is no need for controls over the practice of medicine, including experimental medicine, since it is always conducted in good faith. Or it might be felt that any controls which we institute would unnecessarily hamper the practice of medicine by allowing those not knowledgeable in medical science to discuss technical matters in an invasive way and thus impede medical progress. Do we therefore actually need to control medical experimentation in any way?

Quite apart from the general value of accountability in all professional practice, it may be naïve to assume that professionals always act in good faith. There are some, although relatively few, cases where it has been clear that good faith was not employed in the practice of medicine, and there can be few areas where the pressures on doctors are so great as this area, since discoveries and advances may not only be beneficial to future or present patients but may also further the career of the individual doctor.

There are at least two possible viewpoints which would tend to support a certain amount of control. First, there is the argument from the patient/volunteer. This takes primary account of the need to protect the integrity of the human subject and requires some reliable form of scrutiny to ensure that the balance between the interests of medical progress and the well-being of the research subject is properly maintained. Further, there is the factor of community interests which dictates that the community has some kind of control over experimentation as a means of ensuring that it serves its perceived interests either on a general or a particular level.

Both of these arguments are, however, potentially vulnerable to the kinds of claims, discussed elsewhere,[30] which are made about the nature of medical decision-making. However, even if we accept the argument that the major constituent of all decisions taken in medicine is a purely or primarily medical one, technical incompetence does not necessarily preclude our comments on these decisions. The fact that an individual cannot understand the technicalities of a procedure, does not preclude him from having informed opinions on the need for it or on the value of its anticipated outcome. Further, the general nature of our dependence on health is such that everyone has a legitimate interest in both the practice and the aims of medicine which performs a social as well as a scientific role in the community.

Doctors themselves may argue against the claim that external scrutiny of their decision-making is beneficial. Nevertheless, while accepting that those unqualified in medicine may have only a limited role to play in the day-to-day practice of medicine, we should bear in mind that history can show a number of examples of the excesses to which medicine may go. We have seen that the body of international agreements arose in protest at just such excesses. Indeed, the case of the Nazi doctors highlights the benefits of international control in this area, since the representatives of the community in this example either encouraged or at least did not discourage the practices which were subsequently condemned. We cannot therefore assume that national control will be the only or the most efficient way to ensure the moral acceptability of the medical enterprise. Professional and international commitments may sometimes prove to be more influential than legislative or other intervention.

It is, however, not only the Nazi doctors who have carried out experiments which have subsequently been condemned either nationally or internationally. The use of patients as experimental subjects is particularly commonly abused where the patient is actually incapacitated in a way which makes him vulnerable, for example in the case of children or the terminally or chronically ill. While one can appreciate the aims of the doctor where they are indeed to effect cures, the need to control experimentation becomes clear when we consider that projects which were both outrageous and unscientific have occurred outwith wars and regimes of overt immorality. The injecting of handicapped children with viral hepatitis or chronically ill patients with live cancer cells are only two examples of how the vulnerable may be exploited.[31] While international statements may clearly reject as unethical such experiments, national control may be essential to ensuring that they do not occur, or that where they do there is proper legal redress. In any event, local and international scrutiny of experimentation also serves a symbolic purpose in ensuring that the researcher himself has to consider deeply the ethics and validity of his proposed research project, and thus reminding him of his professional commitments to the subject.

Consent and Experiments

It is not simply the use and potential abuse of experiments which gives rise to concern. While the type of experiment carried out is of fundamental moral importance, the subject's rights in respect of his own body must also be protected. The experimenter is dealing with human subjects, whose rights to autonomy and self-determination may be threatened by an excessive zeal for the development of new therapies and techniques. Protection of these rights involves a perspective of the individual and medicine which 'presupposes some agreement on the nature of human beings.'[32] Whether or not we actually value human life and its attributes absolutely, we nonetheless do have a system of controls, such as the rules about consent and the inbuilt aversion to exploitation, by which doctors are nonetheless bound. The law makes no overtly special rules for hospitals or doctors.

Thus, any experimentation which is carried out is subject not simply to the professional checks which are now built into the legal and professional systems of most advanced societies, but some are also subject to the common law rules about negligence. Moreover, all medical intervention, experimental or not, is further controlled by the common law requirement that the consent of the patient or subjects is necessary, in most cases, to validate the interaction.[33] The problems of the provision of consent are discussed elsewhere, but they are particularly acute when the nature of the intervention is experimental. As has been said:

> The ideal moral and ethical expectations from clinical research scientists are that they should enforce the principles of 'informed consent'...and accept that initial consent becomes void when side effects are potentially or overtly harmful.[34]

However, despite international agreements relating to the voluntary and informed nature of consent, and even despite the individual efforts of a given doctor to obtain such a consent, this consent can never be fully informed in experimental procedures since ex hypothesi the nature and extent of the risk is unknown. Thus, the patient who 'consents' in such circumstances, often does not actually consent to the nature of the risk which may occur, but merely to an incalculable risk worked out on predictions based on pre-existing knowledge or experience. The need to provide consent can, however, serve two purposes in the experimental situation. First, the symbolic one of reminding the researcher of the nature of his subject, and secondly the disclosure which is required to validate consent may involve the researcher in a re-statement of his aims in carrying out the experiment and a re-evaluation of the risks of the enterprise.

There are further problems involved in the obtaining of consent in experiments. It is only possible to argue in a limited number of situations that consent is _freely_ given in the widest sense of the word, particularly in therapeutic research projects where the patient has a self-interest in the cure or the possibility of relief. The nature of the self-interest in, for example, the terminally ill patient is such as to make the consent at least questionable in this respect. However, if the patient is always pressurised in therapeutic experimentation, does this mean that the only subject for research who can give free consent is the volunteer for medical research who is otherwise healthy, but merely concerned to further the aims of medical science or medical knowledge in a non-therapeutic experiment? Or should the fact that all consent in such circumstances is inadequately informed mean that legal rules would prevent the involvement of anyone in experimentation?

This would clearly be an undesirable stance to adopt, since it would absolutely preclude advances in medicine which _are_ beneficial to us as individuals or as groups. The fact that someone is self-interested, however, does not necessarily make his consent invalid. Equally, it might be felt that, although consent may be provided on the basis of inadequate information, the general good of experimentation overrides the diminution in the right to receive information which the patient could otherwise claim. In any event, in the case of the ill patient involved in a therapeutic experiment it could be claimed that, where other therapy has failed, to interfere with his choice to take advantage of an option which at least on current scientific thinking has a chance of success, is more unacceptable than modifying our extreme position on the rights of the individual. The fact that we may justify this type of consent however, does not remove from it the fundamental problem that 'The main ethical problem concerning controlled studies is...not the risk involved but the difficulty in not violating the patient's integrity'.[35]

We have seen that the healthy volunteer for non-therapeutic medical research may in some ways be consenting more freely than the person who consents 'in his own interests' to experimental techniques. However, there are certain groups, who otherwise have the legal capacity to consent, but who are conventionally deemed to be precluded from consenting to participation in research. Thus it is generally felt that prisoners are unsuitable or inappropriate subjects for non-therapeutic research since they may be not be freely consenting. This assessment of their lack of freedom to consent is tied up with the notion that they may be self-interested, i.e. they may be overly influenced by the likelihood of some benefit to themselves in consenting to this type of project. Thus, it would seem that their self-interest, which does not invalidate consent in 'therapeutic' experiments may preclude their participation in non-therapeutic research. But on what grounds? If self-interest does not invalidate consent in some cases, and since consent is always speculative in experimental cases, then could not the self-interest of the prisoner in say, a reduced sentence or a few weeks in hospital, nonetheless leave his consent as valid as that of the patient whose life might literally hinge on the success of the experiment?

The main reason for excluding such groups is of course their vulnerability to exploitation. This consideration is fundamental to all legal or moral exclusions from non-therapeutic experimental programmes, such as in the case of children and the insane. The particular vulnerability of these groups makes control over experimental procedures imperative.

Conclusion

Whatever the type of experiment contemplated, and whoever may be the research subject, a fundamentally important aspect of all experimentation must be the right of the patient/subject to make informed decisions about his own body. The doctor's role as investigator is secondary to the interest which we have in our own autonomy. Potentially this places the patient in a relatively powerful position in respect of experiments and particularly in the assessment of the need for, or morality of, each programme. However, it is often suggested that this role is inappropriate to the patient given his lack of scientific and technical knowledge, and that:

> The basic rule ought to be that the doctor in charge should be entrusted with the duty of himself deciding when a medical care measure needs to be evaluated from an ethical viewpoint.[36]

It would seem, however, that this places too much emphasis on the doctor or researcher and is an unacceptable reduction of the rights of the patient whose interests have already been subverted to some extent, even in therapeutic experiments, by the lack of available information. A balance is necessary which allows for the continuation of that research which is actually or potentially beneficial without ignoring the rights or status of the human subject. We must attempt to ensure that, while benefiting from medical advances and accepting the necessary risks involved, the basic rights which it is claimed all (or at least most) human beings have are not subverted by the interests of medical science in increasing its armoury (however effective).

While it may be true that a certain amount of experimentation is unnecessary or non-beneficial, and that almost all of it is carried out without proper 'informed' consent, it is surely too extreme to abandon all research programmes, some of which have produced palliatives and others undoubted cures. In other words, might we not by means of the kinds of controls over the nature and the ethics of experiments nonetheless continue with those which _may_ or do benefit humanity as a whole, even at the risk of reducing the individual's claims to autonomy which might seem at first sight to preclude experimentation in many situations? Indeed, not all experiments or advances need be precluded on moral grounds, since there are:

> perfectly respectable ethical theories which, in the context of harsh choices....allow for conduct which will benefit the larger or more worth number, even if this inevitably means that others may suffer.[37]

In other words, although arguments from the individual may seem to limit unreasonably the scope of experimentation there are other arguments which might modify an otherwise extreme stance. For example, any perceived need for medical advances might be justified on the ground that it will provide benefits for 'the greatest number'; the moral criterion of rightness in the classical utilitarian model. On utilitarian grounds we may be able to justify even invasive new therapy on the basis that it will maximise the potential for happiness and well-being even of those not directly involved in the experiment. The utilitarian model also allows that measures of this type may be applied where there is no real consent to the risks inherent in the procedure since it may be validated by the claims of the greatest number, or perhaps even by the fact that a risk/benefit analysis shows a balance in favour of benefit. This approach, if combined with our previous claims that experimentation should be limited to that which is non-repetitive and is not solely motivated by commercial or career considerations, could provide the kinds of limitations we have sought in respect of research which is not designed or expected to have immediate benefits for mankind, and could also rule out the types of experiment which provoked the response of international law.

But would this model effectively allow the use of those such as children, and the mentally ill, for 'non-therapeutic' experiments? Where such experiments could be said to be in the interests of the majority, then it is possible that the utilitarian model strictly applied could justify them. This, however, could lead us to a morally dubious position since there are reasons for wanting to preclude, or at least substantially to limit, the use of these groups as experimental subjects. Such grounds include the general moral interest of the community in not exploiting the vulnerable, as well as arguments regarding the need to be legally capable of giving consent. Lack of experience and the inability to understand the implications of the proposed procedure are generally the main reasons given for precluding the provision of legally valid consent in these groups.

However, it nonetheless remains the case that new drugs and therapies may require to be tested on a particular target group, and that therapeutic experiments may have to be conducted on the otherwise vulnerable. This too is a reduction of the protection which these groups might otherwise expect, since their consent cannot be given.

Proxy consent is necessary in such cases, and seems to be generally morally acceptable in the interests of the individual. For example, a cure for the diseases of childhood is unlikely to be found where the subjects used are all adult and by definition do not suffer from the disease in question, or suffer different effects from it. If we are to seek such cures, then some therapeutic and perhaps even non-therapeutic research may be necessary. But can this be justified? Certainly it may be justified by the tenets of utilitarianism as benefiting the greatest number, even where it may deny to a small number the rights which have been described as fundamental. But this also requires the careful assessment of the risks and benefits involved. Our model would not, and could not, be used as a justification for extreme or outrageous risk-taking.

What then can we conclude about experiments? One possible view is that adequate protection is afforded to us when we are sufficiently involved in the decision-making processes of medicine and its related industries to ensure that experiments which have no reasonable hope of benefit to anyone are not carried out, and that the benefits of the therapy or product outweigh the anticipated risks to the experimental subject. This requires that medicine and the public work hand in hand. While the calculation of risks and benefits may at one level be scientific or technical, it also contains a moral or ethical component in the evaluation of the significance of the anticipated benefits and potential harms. As Illich says, 'Medicine is a moral enterprise and therefore inevitably gives content to good and evil.'[38]

If we do not subscribe so wholeheartedly to the idea that 'new' automatically equates with 'good' in medicine, then we may appropriately seek to limit the type and the extent of experimentation and also rule out the offensive and distasteful type of experiment which led to the Declaration of Helsinki. Were this to be achieved it would become less important that the groups involved in the experimental programmes are tightly delimited. Limitations may rather be sought from an informed analysis of the intended outcome, the invasiveness of the treatment, the medical and emotional interests of the subject and the likely risks.

On this model, the nature of experimentation would be more efficiently controlled, although the categories of those who may form the subjects of an experimental programme may be increased in the interests of the community as a whole. As Ajayi[39] has said, we should ideally expect from the experimenter that he should 'avoid inflicting mental and physical suffering [and] guarantee that observed benefits outweigh inherent risks...'[40] Moreover, particular scrutiny is appropriate where the benefits are more those of the community at large than of the subjects of the experiments. The involvement of the community, the reduction of certain types of experimentation and a general moral overview of risks and benefits could contribute to a reflection of the interests of both medicine and patients, and would permit a close scrutiny of the 'need' for experiments and a more careful analysis of the risks and benefits which we may reasonably expect from medical progress.

The application of strictly utilitarian principles to experimentation would, however, give rise to the sacrifice of the interests of the few to those of the many. This is one reason why rights theorists object to utilitarianism. The objection is muted where the minority consents to make the sacrifice, but is more forceful where the subjects cannot give consent, perhaps because they are children or insane. To apply utilitarian reasoning to this situation may appear to have unacceptable results in that it may lead to exploitation. However, where the tenets of utilitarianism are supplemented by a strict application of the principles of consent, and by a restriction on the types and extent of experimentation which are acceptable, then its general principles may provide a satisfactory account of a morally acceptable approach to human experimentation. This would serve the interests which both medicine and the community have in medical progress, and also protect the rights to autonomy and dignity which the human subject may claim.

NOTES

1.   Illich, I., Limits to Medicine. Medical Nemesis: The Expropriation of Health, Harmondsworth, Penguin Books, 1977 edition at p. 255.

2.   This Oath was restated in the Declaration of Geneva in 1947. This up-dated version contains the commitments that:

'I solemnly pledge to consecrate my life to the service of humanity.

I will practice my profession with conscience and dignity.

The health of my patient will be my first consideration.'

3. Declaration of Helsinki 1964, revised in 1975, I (1).

4. Illich, op.cit., at p. 225.

5. Pellegrino, E., and Thomasma, D., A Philosophical Basis of Medical Practice, O.U.P., 1981, at p. viii.

6. Illich, op.cit., at p. 254.

7. Klass, A., There's Gold in Them Thar Pills, Harmondsworth, Penguin Books, 1975, at p. 31.

8. For further discussion, see the 'Sunday Times' 2 March 1980 and 21 September 1980; 'The Guardian' 22 December 1980.

9. Kennedy, I., The Unmasking of Medicine, London, George Allen & Unwin, 1981.

10. ibid., at p. 38.

11. Klass, op.cit., at p. 29.

12. See chapter 10, infra.

13. op.cit.

14. ibid., at p. 30.

15. ibid., at p. 23.

16. For further discussion, see Teff, H., and Munro, C., Thalidomide: The Legal Aftermath, Saxon House, 1976.

17. Pellegrino and Thomasma, op.cit., at pp. viii-ix.

18. For further discussion, see chapter 8, infra.

19. 1955 S.C. 200.

20. For further discussion, see chapter 9, infra.

21. Illich, op.cit., at pp.13-14.

22. Kennedy, op.cit., at p. 152.

23. For some examples, see Katz, J., Experimentation with Human Beings, New York, Russell Sage Foundation, 1972.

24. Kennedy, op.cit., at p. 151.

25. For further discussion, see chapter 5, supra.

26. Established by the Medicines Act 1968. The Committee on Safety of Medicines replaced the Committee on Safety of Drugs (Dunlop Committee).

27. See, for example, 'Concerning Responsibility in Research Investigations on Human Subjects' R.C.P.S. (Glasgow), May 1972.

28. 'Responsibility in Investigations on Human Subjects' Brit. Med. J., 1963, iv., at pp.177-8.

29. Thompson, I.E., et.al., 'Research Ethical Committees in Scotland' Brit.Med. J. 28 February 1981, 718; see also 282 Brit.Med. J., 21 March 1981.

30. See chapter 10, infra.

31. See, Katz, op.cit.

32. Pellegrino and Thomasma, op.cit., at p. x.

33. For further discussion, see chapter 5, supra.

34. Ajayi, O.O., 'Taboos and Clinical Research in West Africa' J.Medical Ethics, 1980, 6, 61.

35. Giertz, G., 'Ethics of randomised clinical trials' J.Medical Ethics, 1980, 6, 55, at p. 56.

36. id.

37. Kennedy, op.cit., at p. 50.

38. op.cit., at p. 53.

39. loc.cit.

40. at p. 61.

7 Sterilisation and Contraception

'The struggle for reproductive self-determination is one of the oldest projects of humanity, one of our earliest collective attempts to alter the biological limits of our existence.'[1]   Man, and particularly, woman, has long sought to achieve the ability and claim the right freely and voluntarily to reproduce.   The interest in protecting such a right has long been given legitimate recognition with the right to reproduce being viewed as a human right.   Indeed it was recently restated as a fundamental human right in the European Declaration of Human Rights.[2]   In the nature of fundamental rights, while they may be alienable, this cannot be done without the consent or volition of the party concerned.

The exercise of the right to reproduce has, however, been fraught with problems.   Efforts have been made to reduce or modify our right to reproduce for a variety of different reasons.   Further, even if we have a right to reproduce, the exercise and existence of that right, while not synonymous with, is nonetheless dependent on, the ability to reproduce.   Perhaps for this reason modern medicine has become intensely involved with providing this ability for those who cannot naturally reproduce, by the development of techniques such as artificial insemination and in vitro fertilisation.   Also, since our attitude to reproduction, and any rights which we may claim in respect of it, depend as much on our ethical beliefs as they do on our biological capacities, it is important that any discussion takes account also of any rights which we may have to control reproduction by means of contraception.   Finally, account must be taken of the interest which other groups may have in our exercise or control of our reproductive capacities.

The Nature and Extent of the Right to Reproduce

The debates which have arisen around the claim that there is a fundamental right to reproduce have centred on the voluntary exercise of this right and the interests of the state or other groups in controlling the reproductive practices of groups or individuals.[3] A contingent debate has arisen round the extent to which we may control our fertility. These debates draw heavily on religious or moral attitudes for their derivation and content.

A full and fundamental right to reproduce exists only where there can be control over the exercise of such a right. This necessarily involves an element of choice which requires individual control over reproductive practices. It has been agreed at an international level that there is a right voluntarily to control reproduction,[4] and that the upholding of this right cannot depend solely on abstinence. This means that the full exercise of the right to reproduce might, in these terms, involve free access to and use of contraception, since people participate in heterosexual intercourse for reasons other than the desire to reproduce. Hence, the development of contraceptive devices has become a feature of contemporary medicine.

If we accept that a necessary corollary of having a right to reproduce is that we have a right to control the exercise of that right, then this must include the option not to use it at all. Thus adults may choose to remain childless whether as a result of abstinence or as the result of using efficient contraception, including sterilisation.

Sterilisation may be used either on medical or on purely birth control grounds. While other forms of birth control are available, in some countries at least, it is now claimed that sterilisation has become one of the most popular ways of controlling reproduction,[5] presumably because of its relative certainty. While much of the debate about sterilisation centres on its enforced use, there has nonetheless been a controversy about whether or not it can legally be carried out voluntarily. These arguments have drawn on religious or moral arguments about the implications of 'maiming', or views about the extent of control which man should have over his biological capacity to create life.

Some consider the right to reproduce primarily from the standpoint of those presently unborn, who are said to have an interest in the reproductive capacity being used. In legal terms while it is difficult to make enforceable such so-called interests on the part of the unborn, rights of action have been granted, by use of legal fiction and doctrine, to those whose interest in being born healthy can be damaged or reduced by the negligent behaviour of others.[6] Even in legal terms then it is not entirely fatuous to talk of the unborn having interests (as distinct, however, from rights), but it seems odd to think of the interests of those who ex hypothesi will never come into existence.

Traditionally the religious input into the debate arises either at the stage at which contraception is used or at the stage of conception. Thus, some religions view mechanical intervention with the lottery that is conception as being a sin, on the grounds that the ability to reproduce is God-given and thus man may not interfere with its exercise. This means that when we talk of a human right to reproduce, we are essentially viewing our reproductive capacities as being subject to use or to total abstinence, and that we cannot have certain choices about when to be fertile while continuing to engage in sexual intercourse. To make the right to reproduce derivative from the God-given power to reproduce, to some extent denies to procreation the full status of a right and views it rather as an ability or perhaps even a duty. These types of arguments are also used when the question of termination of pregnancies is contemplated, since life is God-given also, and is seen as beginning meaningfully at the moment of conception.[7]

For those who espouse such views, sterilisation is also precluded both on grounds of its contraceptive results and also because it is an unwarranted usurpation of control by man over his body. Thus:

> Catholic thought regards sterilisation as a mutilation which deprives the person of a normal vital function of his body and being. It is considered grave and immoral conduct unless carried out in the interests of the health of the whole body.[8]

It is therefore not the sterilisation per se which offends, but rather the results of the operation. These views are concerned with the reason for the sterilisation rather than centring on the operation itself. Thus, interfering with the ability to reproduce can be tolerated only where its use is for the purpose of saving the life of the mother, a type of argument which can invoke the doctrine of double effect in order to find moral justification for the foreseeable results of an operation which will result in sterilisation.[9]

This view of sterilisation is, however, not held by all religions. Thus it is said that:

> Protestant opinion does not denounce sterilisation per se...voluntary sterilisation is considered to be a proper subject for the individual's free exercise of choice and responsibility, functions claimed to be necessary to any concept of morality.[10]

This approach coincides with that adopted by most secular moralists. From some moral positions, then, reproduction is viewed as a biological imperative, whose moral significance depends on its divine source while others would see it as a natural part of the human condition which presents us with the opportunity for the exercise of choice. However, these diverse views lead to fundamental agreement on the question of compulsory removal of reproductive capacity, for while they may differ on the voluntary surrender of the ability to procreate, both would proscribe the compulsory removal of the ability to procreate on distinct, but not mutually exclusive, grounds.

The Legal View

Legal consideration of the right to reproduce has been rare in the United Kingdom, and where it has arisen, it has often been as part of a different aspect of the law, for example in actions concerning nullity of marriage or divorce. Thus questions have been raised as to whether or not the voluntary surrender of reproductive capacity without the knowledge of the spouse or in advance of a marriage, affects the legal status of that marriage. This point was under consideration in the case of Bravery v. Bravery,[11] and provided an opportunity for the judiciary to consider the question of whether or not voluntary sterilisation is lawful and if certain types of control can be exercised over our right to reproduce.

This case also provided the judges with the opportunity to express their own religious or political stance in the course of justifying their decision. For example, Lord Denning in referring to the practice of voluntary sterilisation was clearly influenced by his ideas of sexual morality and his views of the public interest as much as by matters of fundamental rights. In the course of his judgment, and as a basis for his decision, he presented the following picture for consideration:

> Take a case where a sterilisation operation is done so as to enable a man to have the pleasure of sexual intercourse without shouldering the responsibilities attaching to it. The operation then is plainly injurious to the public interest. It is degrading to the man himself. It is injurious to his wife and any woman he may marry, to say nothing of the way it opens to licentiousness; and, unlike contraceptives, it allows no room for a change of mind on either side. It is illegal, even although the man consents to it...[12]

Clearly, although the point about reversibility is well made, it is not one of fundamental importance, i.e. even were medicine able to reverse the operation it would have little effect on the central theme of judgments of this type which relate to the idea – which has some affinity with some of the religious views already mentioned – that there is about the ability to procreate almost the air of a duty rather than a right, or at least that responsibility should be taken for sexual pleasures. Indeed, this judgment could well have been extended to other (reversible) forms of contraception.

The application of strictly legal, as opposed to moral, principle led, however, to a different conclusion in the above case, and tended to support the claim that man as a moral agent may indeed control his reproductive capacities without rendering himself liable at least to legal condemnation even where the operation is carried out for reasons purely of birth control. The law therefore in the United Kingdom would seem to support the right to control reproduction, although Courts have not often been asked to consider the existence or protection of the right to reproduce.

Although consideration of such matters has been rare, it would appear that the law is not prepared to consider sterilisation voluntarily entered into as a criminal offence. Gordon[13] has in fact claimed that, at least under Scots law, for sterilisation to be unlawful it would be necessary to create a new offence.[14] Indeed, advances in the understanding of the genetic transmission of disease lead logically to the conclusion that some affected families may see sterilisation as the only manageable way of ensuring that their reproductive capacity is so controlled as to ensure that no pregnancies, or further pregnancies, occur, so that sterilisation may be seen as one of the logical outcomes of an efficient screening programme for genetic defects.[15] This does not mean that it might not form the basis of, for example, a civil action for divorce where the ability of one party to reproduce is removed without the consent of the other, if this affects the health of the second party. In this respect, sterilisation stands on the same footing as other contraceptive practices.[16]

Further, while it makes little sense to talk of a right to reproduce where the biological capacity to do so is absent, the capacity can be viewed as prospective and therefore worthy of protection. Thus, acceptance that there is a fundamental right to reproduce logically precludes the compulsory removal of the capacity to reproduce even where it cannot biologically be exercised, for example in the case of the very young, or in cases where its use would be proscribed by the law on other grounds, such as in the case of those below the age of consent. One case where this subject was under consideration was the case of Re D (a minor).[17] In this case, a mother sought to have her young daughter sterilised on the grounds that her mental handicap made her vulnerable to sexual exploitation and that she therefore ran a high risk of unwanted pregnancies. While the mother obtained the consent of the medical personnel to the carrying out of the operation, another concerned non-medical expert, sought to challenge the authority to proceed with the surgery.

The court was asked to consider whether or not there was a fundamental, and therefore protectable, right to reproduce. Interestingly, despite the fact that the right to reproduce may be circumscribed, as in this case, by rules concerning age, such artificial considerations were not effective in the major concern of the court which was with the protection of the potential exercise of rights.

In the event, the court made reference to the fundamental right to reproduce in deciding that the sterilisation operation could not go ahead. While not doubting the good faith of the mother, the implication of the judgment was that decisions about alienating fundamental rights were not appropriately taken by a third party, however closely concerned, at least where the person in question would be in a position to exercise their right in the future. The decision therefore cannot be taken as an absolute authority for the claim that such rights cannot be alienated, nor for the claim that they cannot be alienated by third parties acting in the interests of the incapax. What the decision does do, however, is to reinforce the claim that a fundamental right does exist, and to reassert the fact that rights will be protected even where their exercise is potential rather than actual.

Further, and this may seem to point to the right's dependence on the availability of choice and control, it was also noted that pregnancy could be avoided by the use of other methods such as contraception, or, if not avoided then at least terminated. So the court was not disputing the undesirability, at least in the short term, of conception, but rather stressed the importance of the ability to procreate being protected. It is not therefore the restriction on procreation which was fundamental, but rather the ability to retain the use of the choice for possible exercise in the future. What is particularly interesting about this decision is that the general prohibition of the criminal law in respect of the act of intercourse taking place under certain ages, was a mere side-consideration. The use of contraceptives other than sterilisation was accepted as a possibility, the prohibition on compulsory sterilisation relating therefore to considerations other than the legality of the exercise.

Limitations on the Right to Control Reproduction

Whether or not there is a fundamental human right to control reproduction, and it might seem that this is an essential corollary of the right to reproduce, there is at least an internationally agreed legal right to do so. However, as with all rights, this may be limited where certain justifications can be provided. The right to life, for example, surely the most fundamental which we may claim, can be restricted by due process of law where for example countries retain the death penalty. Normally, the limitation of such rights is justified by an overriding interest on the part of the community. This will also be true therefore of the right to reproduce or to control reproduction.

Certainly the community does have an interest in the reproductive practices of its members. Thus, rules have grown up surrounding the practice of abortion, which serve to limit and define the legality of the operation itself, and provide a means of reflecting the moral tone of the community as well as protecting the interests or prospective rights of the unborn child.[18] Situations such as this have a clear application to the control of reproduction by other means, although some of the issues may be different. While the abortion debate often centres on the question of killing, the debate about contraception (including sterilisation) will centre rather on moral objections to the practice or the interests of the state in controlling the ability to reproduce. Indeed, it is sometimes claimed that the restrictions which have grown up around women's claims to have a right to terminate a pregnancy may also reflect the interests of the state. Thus where illegal abortion is a major contributor to maternal death there may be a legitimate interest on the part of the state to legalise it within certain areas. Equally, the fact that birth rates may fall with the increasing availability of legal termination may cause a corresponding community interest in limiting the availability of terminations.

In considering both reproduction and its control, the question of the extent and the legitimacy of the state's interest in and control over the use to which we put our fundamental right, has an important place. Of course, an element of state control in our lives is an inevitable part of our social and political structures. Neither is the use of medical techniques in that intervention unusual. In questions of reproduction, however, the skills of medicine may become a tool in a fundamentally invasive programme to enforce the removal of basic human rights. Further, the development of more acceptable and reliable forms of contraception, while a laudable medical aim, may be discarded by the state in the interests of maintaining a high level of reproduction or as a means of reinforcing religious dogma.

The different aims of medicine and politics are never more clear than when the right to reproduce and the right to control fertility are under consideration. The role played by the law, however, in the resolution of aims and goals, has historically been relatively minimal in the United Kingdom, largely due to the fact that seldom has there been an overt challenge to the right to reproduce, or at least seldom have such challenges been discussed by a court of law. Rather the aims of medical science in promoting safe and efficient control of fertility, while at the same time attempting to secure fertility for the infertile couple, have paralleled the interest of the law in safeguarding the development of the full potential of the individual. Indeed, the law's only major incursion into reproductive practices is the case of abortion, and in this case the interests under consideration differ fundamentally. The competing interests of the unwilling mother and the interest of the state in not countenancing the killing of prospective citizens have been partially resolved by a (fairly restrictive) balancing process.

While courts in the United Kingdom have been wary of seeming to support the right to control reproduction after conception, this question has been overtly considered by American courts. In Roe v. Wade[19] for example, the right to take decisions about reproduction, even after conception, was seen as an aspect of the right of the individual to privacy, a right guaranteed by the United States Constitution. However, the right was not absolute since the court equally claimed that it may, at certain stages in the pregnancy, be limited by the legitimate interest of the State either in the life of the developing child and/or in the health of the mother. Therefore absolute rights to decide about termination of pregnancies were granted only up to the end of the first trimester of the pregnancy, limited rights in the second trimester, and finally the interests of the state were deemed to overrule the wishes of the mother in the final trimester. This case illustrates that 'Although human rights are, in theory at least, not defeated by an appeal to the common interest they might, of course, have to yield to other human rights where these come into conflict.'[20] Thus, for example, the stage of the pregnancy where the rights of the foetus may conflict with the right of the mother to terminate the pregnancy, could provide the focal point of arguments about the time-limit for abortion being lawfully carried out.[21]

Considerations in Control

The fundamental right to reproduce is one which is safeguarded by the law in most states, even where economic or demographic reasons might seem to indicate that the compulsory control of reproduction would more closely serve the interests of the community as a whole.   In situations where the state attempts to override the autonomy of the individual, such as recent events in India where economic and political constraints might logically support the programmes of sterilisation which were carried out, the reaction to these schemes was the universal condemnation of the government.

As we have seen, 'As a human right it [the right to reproduce] exercises some sort of exclusionary power over arguments based on public convenience and expense.'[22]   The interest of the state therefore would require to be compelling before the right to reproduce could be limited.   To maintain that there is a fundamental protectable right to reproduce, therefore, is not to say that it can never be interfered with since '...even the most precious rights are not absolute'.[23]   However, the limitations which are put on the right to reproduce must, if the human right is to mean anything, correspond to a perceived and paramount need, perhaps found in the interests of others, to control fertility.

States have chosen to exercise some control over the reproductive rights of their citizens on a variety of grounds and in a number of different ways.   We have seen that it may be an essential constituent of the exercise of a right that we have a reasonable alternative to its exercise, which may imply the right to control reproduction in ways which stop short of the suppression of human sexuality by means of abstinence.   Equally, it has been claimed that the nature of a fundamental human right is such that, while it may be limited, this can only be justified where the right of A actually conflicts with the right of others to exercise fundamental human rights.   Limitations have also arisen out of moral views which are deemed to be held by the majority of a given community.

Almost all legal systems, generally through the use of the criminal rather than the civil law, have proscribed, and continue to proscribe, sexual relationships between people who are related to certain degrees, in some cases by marriage but more commonly by consanguinity. Although the laws have changed over the years and have become less restrictive, they nonetheless forbid sexual intercourse between certain individuals. While this does not preclude the actual mechanical ability to reproduce, nonetheless it effectively limits the choice of partner in much the way that there is a form of limitation on marriage in the United States represented by the compulsory analysis of blood tests in advance of marriage. These prohibitions of incest, while generally contemporarily justified on genetic grounds (which are only convincing where procreation is a possibility) are also partly based on religious tradition and moral views on the nature of the family.[24]

Equally, the law may effectively remove from certain groups the right to reproduce, at least temporarily, by laws which render intercourse unlawful, for example, in respect of those under the legal age of consent. Such decisions as setting age limits on the right to exercise control over one's own body tend to be based rather on historical intuitions than on observable criteria relating to the effect on other people's rights. Thus, the justification for such rules cannot be those overriding interests which we have claimed may be used to limit the exercise of fundamental rights, but is rather based on predictions about the suitability of or success of, the individual parenting. However, a purpose may be served in a general way by the imposition of limitations in that the vulnerable may be protected from exploitation. There can be no doubt that this is a fundamental consideration of the law, and seen in this perspective, whether or not one may wish to argue about the actual age which is set, it should be clear that the intervention of the state is legitimately paternalistic in the interest of its members.

In any event, to deny the right to make entirely unfettered decisions about with whom to procreate, or at what age to procreate, does not serve to reduce the status of the right to reproduce. Limitation of choice can be justified on considerations which in no way impinge on the protection which the law will give to our basic rights. Thus, while it may be important that we can control or retain our capacity to reproduce, it may equally be important in the interests of others that the right to reproduce is exercised within certain defined boundaries. For as long as these boundaries are relatively wide, our freedom of choice is only marginally limited. The power of the state is, therefore, legitimately exercised in such cases. Since restrictions of this sort reflect on the choice of partner or on the moral condemnation of the community, they therefore do not actually make our right vulnerable in any sense.

On what other grounds then might the state or groups within states want to limit the right of the individual to exercise control over their right to reproduce? Some would for example claim that the individual interest in controlling (and particularly in limiting) reproduction shows direct parallels with the rise of the women's movement. Vested interests might therefore wish to ensure that such reproductive self-determination becomes difficult, if not unlawful, on grounds which owe little to the religious or moral considerations already discussed, and nothing to the conflict with the rights of others, but rather to the desire to control the role of women in economic and political life. Other reasons may be purely religious or may reflect the perceived moral interests or needs of the community such as those already discussed in respect of termination of pregnancies.

Reproduction and its control are obvious focal points for political, economic and eugenic control of certain groups whose reproduction is not deemed to be appropriate or desirable. Control of this type has traditionally been achieved by the device of involuntary or non-voluntary sterilisation, although, as has been seen, control may also be attempted through the voluntary surrender of the right and the ability to reproduce by the use of moral or religious arguments.

Eugenic Arguments

Elementary understanding of genetics has been used, both as a device whereby people may opt for or against reproduction, and, more insidiously, as a reason for intrusion into what has been termed the fundamental right of the individual to make certain choices about his/her pre-existing ability to procreate. This latter use of genetic knowledge demonstrates clearly the more sinister side of the debate about choices in reproduction. Genetic knowledge has been used to justify such intrusions with a number of different purposes; eugenic (for instance, improving the genetic stock of the community by refusing to allow known carriers or defectives to reproduce), political and economic (for example the inability or unwillingness of the state to support children born damaged or defective), social (for example, the interest of the state in not having children born into inadequate families) and penological/social (as a means of ensuring the early release of some groups from institutional care and as a form of punishment).

The use of the eugenic argument in such situations has in the past been rife, and still commands a certain amount of support in some places. Our understanding of genetics is such that we have some understanding, if not a complete one, of the means and likelihood of the transmission of certain defects and diseases. Although such arguments continue to be used, there is considerable distaste for them. Indeed, recent experiences in the Second World War have shown that compulsory eugenic sterilisation is by and large greeted with universal condemnation. While we may readily accept that those who are carrying or likely to have damaged or defective offspring should have the option of abortion or sterilisation, the argument becomes qualitatively different when it is used as a justification for compulsory termination of pregnancies or compulsory sterilisation.

Nor can we assume that such arguments are only used by groups which are generally reviled like the Nazis. Experience in sophisticated and generally admired states has shown that the interest of the state in controlling reproduction may well be used there to justify removing this fundamental right from some groups. This may, of course, be achieved in two distinct ways. It may for example, be the result of 'encouraging', in the national interest, certain groups not to reproduce, or of the direct invasion and removal of their rights under compulsory programmes, or of a national or local programme involving the compulsory sterilisation of certain individuals. It has been claimed that it is:

137

rational to encourage sterilisation not only of the mentally abnormal, but other groups of disadvantaged individuals, especially where they can be identified as being likely to produce abnormal children.[25]

Clearly, 'encouragement' may include an element of duress, particularly where it is an authority figure who 'encourages' the individual. However, in theory at least, there remains an element of choice as to whether or not to accept the advice being given. While courts in the United Kingdom, on the rare occasions when the issue has been raised, have not supported either non-voluntary or involuntary sterilisation, this is by no means a universal feature. The propensity of the law to isolate itself from certain types of morality is never more clear than in the statutes which were upheld and deemed supportable in some states in America during this century.[26]

The growth of the eugenic movement was paralleled by the increase in appeals to the improvement of man's lot by the careful and planned control of the genetic pool. This was to be achieved by the limitation, on a compulsory basis if necessary, of the rights of certain individuals or groups to procreate. In their role as upholders and implementers of the law, courts (with no noticeable reluctance) were prepared to interpret such legislation as both constitutional and enforceable. The main thrust of the arguments was directed not just at the powers of the state but also at the interest of the majority in preventing the minority from from spoiling or reducing the quality of the genetic pool of the community. Indeed, the argument based on eugenics places the interests of the community as a whole at a central point. The protection of the 'best interests of the community', while it may be a philosophically uncertain basis for the denial of a basic human right, is nonetheless often central to the role played by courts. Thus, the justification offered in such cases was that:

> ...if there be any natural right for natively mental defectives to beget children, that right gives way to the police power of the State in protecting the common welfare, so far as it can be protected, against this hereditary type of feeble-mindedness.[27]

One further problem with this type of argument is that it is based on inadequate predictive certainties. While it is true that

138

there is an increased risk of the transmission of certain genetic disorders such as haemophilia, (depending on the sex of the child) it is interestingly not in respect of those groups, where prediction is reasonably certain, that such arguments have traditionally been used, but rather against those whose form of 'defect' or 'abnormality' is less certainly transmitted by genes.

The feeble-minded for example, are often, in conjunction with other groups such as prisoners, the main target group of arguments of this sort. The major problem in supporting these arguments is not simply their discriminatory nature, nor even their dubious morality, but also that they represent as definitive genetic predictions which are at best speculative. Thus while the case may be made that the chances of having a handicapped child increase where the parent suffers from the handicap, e.g. the feeble-minded parent may be more likely to produce a feeble-minded child, by no means all feeble-minded children are born to feeble-minded parents. Certainly, it is clear that while the link between the defective parent and the defective child may in some cases be more than merely tenuous, it is not sufficiently strongly predictable to justify the imposition of a ban on reproduction. As has been said:

> The right to marry and the right to bear children are so
> fundamental that a heavy burden of proof should be placed
> on those who claim that society should give special
> priority to the reduction of genetic disease - even
> through programmes that envisage minimal compromise of
> these freedoms.[28]

For such intervention to be justified, it must be based on reasonably certain predictions, and, if there is a fundamental right to reproduce, even that scientific certainty will be insufficient justification for the compulsory removal of that right unless its exercise prevents the exercise by others of their fundamental rights. Thus:

> Compulsory sterilisation might...be compatible with the
> right to reproduce where the exercise of this right
> interferes with the, perhaps more basic, human rights of
> others. Thus, if the actual survival of society was
> threatened by the unlikely occurrence of a rapid genetic
> decline, control of the reproductive process could be
> justified.[29]

139

Equally, the state may declare economic or political interests which, it may be claimed, make it unable or unwilling to care for those born damaged or defective. The use of economic arguments in this area of fundamental importance is, however, generally unappealing. Indeed, despite the necessarily substantial financial commitment which it is necessary for a state to make in caring for the disabled and the handicapped, most states have nonetheless shown themselves to be relatively committed to projects of this sort. Moreover, the state also commits substantial sums of money to detection of disabilities prenatally and to genetic counselling services which provide advice to families at risk and may be able to make informed estimates of the likelihood of disability. Despite the relative accuracy of diagnosing families at risk the state has not seen fit to intervene and enforce termination of pregnancies, or to make sterilisation compulsory even in the knowledge of the financial commitment which may be undertaken in permitting existing pregnancies to continue or allowing for possible future pregnancies. The state's interest in such programmes is therefore the protection of the interests and freedoms of the 'at risk' individual, rather than any hypothetical or real financial interest it may have in not having to care for, or contribute substantially to the care of, the handicapped and disabled.

However, although economic arguments find little mass support in the present day, they have been important in shaping the laws and attitudes of some jurisdictions in the past, for example in some states in America. Indeed some welfare recipients in the U.S.A. have recently been denied the benefits to which they are entitled until they undertook to have no further children. Again, however, the limited certainties of genetic prediction make such a basis for decision-making insupportable, even if one grants it to be morally acceptable in principle. Appeals to the interests of the state, as a justification for overriding the rights of individuals, may seem more convincing where it is known that the threat to the state is real and that only by overriding some individual interests can the state either protect their other fundamental rights or those of others. In any event, a compulsory sterilisation programme would be a highly inefficient means of ensuring that the state is not burdened with those who are handicapped and dependent on it for care and sustenance since the relevant genetic predictions are necessarily uncertain. For these reasons, there can be little doubt that:

> If the major social goal were simply to reduce the amount of money required for the care of persons with severe, incurable genetic disease, the most efficient course would be to adopt a policy favouring infanticide.[30]

Clearly, however, most people would find the imposition of such a scheme intolerable since, regardless of the logic of the approach, many people think that there is a clear difference between aborting a foetus and killing an existing child, even where it is only seconds or minutes separated from its mother's womb.

The 'Right' to Adequate Parenting

The interests of the state may, however, seem emotionally and morally more compelling when they purport to be child-centred. Arguments which depend on the so-called rights of a child to be born into an 'adequate' or caring family may seem at first sight to be less morally objectionable than purely eugenic or economic arguments, since they focus on the rights of the individual rather than on the interests of the state. However, the role of the state is nonetheless of considerable importance to arguments of this sort, since it is the state which will decide what makes a family 'adequate'. Such judgments will inevitably be based on criteria which reflect the wider interests of the state as well as those which concern the happiness or fulfilment of the individual.

However, one strength of this type of argument is that it does not depend on eugenic considerations and therefore is not vulnerable to claims that genetic prediction is uncertain. As Meyers says:

> One eugenic argument for compulsory sterilisation not affected by the present lack of genetic understanding is that the feeble-minded are not capable of rearing healthy offsprings endowed to them and that society and themselves would benefit by preventing the bad effects of children being reared in such unhealthy or undesirable environments.[31]

This argument equally, however, cannot benefit from the claims of the proponents of compulsory sterilisation that it serves to improve the genetic stock of mankind. If the feeble-minded are able (as they statistically are more likely to do than not) to produce healthy children, then random compulsory sterilisation would be an inefficient and short-sighted way of improving the stock of human genetic pools. Equally, where defective offspring are the result, in many cases this would only become evident in the later life of the child, in which case the solution most likely to achieve the desired result would be a programme which sanctioned the killing of all children where, for example, their I.Q. was below that for normal schools.

Of course, some might wish to argue that, since the feeble-minded are not deemed able properly to take care of their children, the lesser of two evils would be not to let them have children even although this involves gambling with the genetic pool, in that we may prevent the birth of substantial numbers of healthy, normal children. Further, it may be argued that the feeble-minded would not notice the removal of the right or the ability to have children by the very nature of their condition. However, we have already seen that to have a human right does not require consciousness of that right nor, as in the case of children, the ability to use it except prospectively.[32] Thus, the comatose patient, who is clearly presently and perhaps permanently unaware of rights which he might have been able to claim in other circumstances, is nonetheless still deemed to possess them. For example, the doctor who denies a right to life to an irreversibly comatose patient is no less guilty of killing that person than is the man who stabs another to death in a fight.

In any event, arguments based on parenting ability are as open to abuse as the other arguments which have been discussed. Not only do they allow for an unwelcome degree of state control in taking decisions about fitness for parenting, but the testing for fitness itself would seem to be in direct confrontation with any claim that there is a fundamental right to reproduce. It has been said that 'The point of establishing rights in general, and human rights in particular, is to protect the individual against being used as an instrument of public policy.'[33] Thus, any but the most minimal test of this type would be precluded by acceptance of the basic right to reproduce, particularly where these arguments are based on merely economic or financial considerations.

Penological/Social Arguments

Compulsory sterilisation may also be used as a technique of punishment, or at least individuals may be coerced into submitting to compulsory sterilisation as a means of avoiding the full rigours of the criminal law. Although this has recently been held to be unconstitutional in the United States,[34] the more common interest in this area has centred on the question of castration, designed to reduce sex drive rather than to preclude reproduction, although of course it may also have that effect where successful. Courts in both Canada and the United Kingdom, while interested in requests for castration from prisoners have nonetheless deemed this to be beyond the scope of the interests of the courts and a matter for the person and his medical advisors alone.[35] This is not to say that the courts are never involved in reducing or removing the right to procreate, but this is generally an indirect result of other considerations.

For example, it is clear that the prisoner and the insane are effectively denied, at least for the period of their incarceration, the right to reproduce since they are segregated according to sex. It may be that the temporary removal of the right to reproduce in such cases (as with the right to vote) is seen as part of the necessary and just punishment by society of wrongdoers. On a substantially discredited, but once relatively influential, school of criminological thought, of course, the denial of the opportunity to exercise the right of reproduction might have seemed justified since it was held that criminality was genetically pre-disposed. In any event, we do sanction in some states and in certain situations the removal of fundamental human rights from certain individuals who have offended the morals of society; indeed the right to legislate for and carry out a death penalty is expressly permitted by the European Declaration on Human Rights.[36]

143

Conclusion

A brief survey of the major reasons given for supporting the use of compulsory sterilisation as a means of controlling reproduction serves to highlight the common and most divisive element which emerges from all theories, whether genetic or political.   This is, that all arguments are essentially discriminatory, quite apart from the fact that they are often based on inadequate information.

This raises further problems which relate to the process of labelling people so as to identify whether or not they are consigned to certain groups such as 'unfit' parents or anti-social personalities.   Indeed, however accurate genetic predictions may become in the future, the question remains as to the legitimate right of any state to disvalue certain lives or prospective lives on the basis of these or any other criteria.   Debates surrounding the death penalty, abortion, euthanasia and the treatment of the elderly, sick and the new-born handicapped have rehearsed the arguments for and against such attitudes being legitimated.   By and large, it would seem that even where some might agree that, in theory, there are some situations where such decisions may be properly made, the potential for outright abuse of the principle will serve to restrict the legitimation of any scheme based on arguments about 'quality of life' and so on.   Whatever the actual results of arguments based on this, or on criteria about the suitability of the individual and the desirability of his/her procreating, it is often said that the labelling process is so suspect as to make major decisions contingent on it morally untenable.   Illich, for example, claims that:

> Any society, to be stable, needs certified deviance.
> People who look strange, or who behave oddly are
> subversive until their common traits have been formally
> named and their startling behaviour slotted into a
> recognised pigeonhole.   By being assigned a name and a
> role, eerie, upsetting freaks are tamed, becoming
> predictable exceptions who can be pampered, avoided,
> repressed or expelled.[37]

While society may depend on this labelling process for these reasons, its recognition as essentially artificial, or at least as potentially erroneous, should reduce its power as an argument for the removal of fundamental rights.

However, to say that such practices would be open to abuse may seem an insufficient reason to preclude their use altogether. This may be particularly so where the decision is taken in situations such as the legalised termination of pregnancies where the child is likely to be severely handicapped. Such decisions are subject to the scrutiny of the law and the second opinion of those involved in the 'moral enterprise' of medicine.[38] However, in such circumstances we are dealing with a separate problem about the rights of the handicapped to be born, rather than with the argument about the legitimacy of compulsion in the choice of reproduction.

In any event, it is not simply the likelihood of abuse which makes programmes of this sort objectionable and inconsistent with the human status. The imposition of compulsion on such grounds is also distasteful because it is discriminatory. Recent examples of this discrimination have been the case of those women who were placed under financial duress by their employers. In the event, several women 'voluntarily' underwent sterilisation operations as a means of retaining their employment.

To say that there is not a convincing argument to support the desire to limit reproduction in certain cases does not of course demonstrate that there could be no such reason. Human rights may be moderated or even denied in some cases. For example, the right of free speech which is guaranteed by constitution or custom in many states is circumscribed by other rules about defamation, public order and so on. If the right to reproduce is a right in this category then it may also be limited on similar socially accepted and acceptable grounds. As we have seen, even if the right to reproduce is a more fundamental one than the right to free speech it may nonetheless also be moderated in the interests of the rest of the community's abilities to exercise other fundamental rights. Certain groups within the community may therefore have their basic rights removed in what is seen as the overwhelming interests of the state, and the prospective right to life may be removed in the interests of the mother where the question is that of the termination of a pregnancy. The interests of the state in intervening in this way must, however, be compelling.

Control of reproduction is therefore not simply a personal or even a medical matter, but has clear political and moral overtones.

This may be true even where what is being argued for is the voluntary control of reproductive capacity. Thus, the struggle of women in states such as the Republic of Ireland for the legitimation of contraception is as much a political as a personal dispute since it challenges the morality reflected by the state and also the constitutional right of the state to legislate on the basis of purely religious dogma.

Where the state attempts to remove from the individual the right to reproduce, the implications are even more overtly political. For a fundamental right to be meaningful, it must also be technically possible (now or in the future) to make use of it and it was consideration of this point which led the court in Re D[39] to refuse to sanction sterilisation which would have taken place otherwise without reference to the wishes of the child concerned. The right may also, however, involve the ability to choose whether or not to exercise it. Thus, we may have a right to life, but may choose to die, either by committing suicide (now decriminalised), and by failing to seek or by refusing consent to life-saving medical treatment. Thus, it may not make sense to talk of a right where those who may claim to have it are actually incapable of exercising it. It would, for example, be unusual to talk of the sterile as having a right to reproduce.

The right to reproduce, if it is fundamental in the sense of being universal, may imply more than simply the right to have children. It can also been seen, perhaps more importantly, as the right not to have reproductive abilities interfered with by, for example, compulsory sterilisation. Seen in this way, it is more than just a biological capacity and more resembles our original claim that it is an important and essential constituent of the human state. Indeed, some communities would seem to have recognised this by sanctioning the development of techniques to ensure that those who cannot reproduce (and therefore are denied certain choices) without assistance, may reasonably expect the availability of that help. There may even be a right to receive medical help to ensure fertility.

What is clear is that the right to reproduce is one which is essential to the personal autonomy of the individual. The full use of this right cannot be dependent on using it rationally, but does imply that a choice exists as to whether or not to use it. Certainly it is fundamental to the autonomy of the individual that he or she can control his or her own reproductive capacity without state or other intervention unless the competing interests of those seeking to interfere with the exercise of that right are sufficiently compelling. This would largely preclude the modification or removal of the right on the basis of suspect criminological theories, uncertain genetic predictions and mere political or economic expedience. As Meyers says:

> There surely must come a point to which medical advances have perhaps already brought us, where society — represented by a legislative majority - no longer has the right to use its knowledge to manipulate and mutilate the bodies of those it fears somehow do not fit the desired social mould.[40]

NOTES

1. Gordon, L., Woman's Body, Woman's Right. Harmondsworth, Penguin Books, 1977, at p. 403.
2. (1953), particularly Article 12 which provides to men and women the right to marry and found a family.
3. See, for example, Hilton, B., et.al., (eds), Ethical Issues in Human Genetics, New York, Plenum Press, 1973.
4. Declaration on Population 1966; the right of parents to determine the number and spacing of their children was also expressly declared at the Teheran International Conference on Human Rights in 1968.
5. Gonzales, B., 'Voluntary Sterilization: Counseling as a prerequisite to Informed Consent', Proceedings of the 5th. World Congress on Medical Law, (1979), at p. 64.
6. Under common law in Scotland, and under the Congenital Disabilities (Civil Liability) Act 1976 in England and Wales.
7. For further discussion, see chapter 2, supra.
8. Meyers, D., The Human Body and the Law, Edinburgh University Press, 1970, at p. 3.
9. For further discussion of the principle of double effect, see chapter 3, supra.
10. Meyers, op.cit., at p. 4.
11. [1954] 3 All E.R. 39.

12. ibid., at p. 68.

13. Gordon, G.H., The Criminal Law of Scotland, (1st Ed.), Edinburgh, W. Green & Son, 1967.

14. ibid., at p. 775. It is further pointed out that the creation of a new criminal offence is unlikely - see The Criminal Law of Scotland, (2nd Ed.), Edinburgh, W. Green & Son, 1978, at pp. 29-43; see also Williams, G., Textbook of Criminal Law, London, Stevens & Sons, 1978, particularly at p. 524.

15. For further discussion on genetic predictions see, Ferguson-Smith, M.A., 'Medical Genetics and the Law', in McLean, S.A.M., (ed), Legal Issues in Medicine, Gower Publishing Co., 1981, 133.

16. See for example, Cackett v. Cackett [1950] P 253; Baxter v. Baxter [1948] A.C. 274; R v. R [1952] 1 All E.R. 1194.

17. [1976] 1 All E.R. 326.

18. For further discussion, see chapter 2, supra.

19. Roe v. Wade 410 U.S. 113 (1973).

20. McLean, S.A.M., and Campbell, T.D., 'Sterilisation' in McLean, S.A.M., op.cit., 176, at p. 182.

21. For further discussion, see chapter 2, supra.

22. McLean and Campbell, loc.cit., at p. 182.

23. Reilly, P., Genetics, Law and Social Policy, Cambridge, Mass., Harvard U.P., 1977, at p. 134.

24. For further discussion, see Lord Kilbrandon, 'The Comparative Law of Genetic Counseling' in Hilton et.al., op.cit., 254.

25. 'Focus', J. Medical Ethics (1975), 1, 163, at p. 164.

26. See for example, the cases of State v. Troutman 50 Idaho 763 (1931); Buck v. Bell 274 U.S. 200 (1927).

27. State v. Troutman, supra cit.

28. Reilly, op.cit., at p. 145.

29. McLean and Campbell, loc.cit., at p. 182.

30. Reilly, op.cit., at p. 145.

31. op.cit., at p. 43.

32. See chapter 4, supra.

33. McLean and Campbell, loc.cit., at p. 182.

34. Skinner v. Oklahoma 316 U.S. 535 (1942).

35. R v. Whiffen [1980] 7 Current Law 39; see also the Canadian case of Regina v. Williams 1 Legal Medical Quarterly 144 (1977).

36. Article 5 (1).

37. Illich, <u>Limits   to   Medicine.   Medical   Nemesis: The
     Expropriation of Health</u>, Harmondsworth, Penguin Books, 1977
     edition, at p. 124.

38. For further discussion, see chapter 2, supra.

39. supra cit.

40. op.cit., at p. 47.

8 Negligence

The raising of an action in negligence by a patient against a doctor is the classic example of the conflict between medicine and its patients. Generally the action signifies disappointment with the therapy chosen or the manner of its delivery and encapsulates the frustration and hostility which the patient may feel when the medicine which he has regarded as his salvation 'lets him down'.

The claims of the medical profession to an exclusive and successful control of medicine and health care lead to the creation of a unique relationship between doctor and patient. Since man aspires to health and the doctor is the typical and predominant representative of healing '...both [the doctor and the patient] are locked in a human relationship the acuteness of which is rarely encountered in day-to-day life.'[1] Not only is the person seeking treatment aware of his dependence on the medical practitioner, but the efficacy of treatment often depends on the establishing of good personal relationships between doctor and patient. This means that the success of medicine as an enterprise depends to an extent on the public image which it creates, both in the general sense of confidence in the discipline as a whole, and more particularly in the sense of the relationship which the individual doctor has with the individual patient. For this reason, patients must be seen as individuals and not merely as symptoms, with doctors as healers reinforcing the trust of the patient and thereby persuading or convincing the patient to participate in the transaction.

The success of modern medicine in convincing the public as to its competence in health matters means that it is not only the individual patient who demonstrates an almost mystical faith in the medical profession. The community has also come to place its trust in the intervention of conventional medicine. The belief that health is a fundamental good has been translated into the belief that medicine is a fundamental good. Clearly, however, although modern medicine may be one way of achieving the health which man desires, it is not by any means the sole way. Diet, exercise, tobacco, alcohol and drugs may be used and abused to limit or protect our health.

Much of contemporary medicine is dependent on the development of new techniques and high technology, but it is not only the scientific aspects of medicine which generate expectations. The high expectations of the patient are created also by the fact that, at its best, medicine is highly personalised.

> Medicine as medicine is...more than a clinical or basic science applied to individual cases. It is a particularised knowledge of prudent human actions, dependent upon scientific methods and art but not synonymous with them.[2]

This personalisation of medicine involves more than a concentration of attention on the personal characteristics of the patient; it involves appraising each individual as a whole person whose thoughts and feelings have significance in themselves, and may contribute to the determination of the appropriate treatment. Thus, the individual patient becomes an important part of the practice of medicine, shaping and altering the techniques and therapies. His consent and understanding are as important to the nature of the interaction as the technical competence of the doctor. 'It would be inappropriate, not to say false, to consider human beings merely collections of organ systems and deposits of disease entities.'[3]

Moreover the patient's anxieties about the nature of the relationship and its outcome (which might result in the raising of a legal action) are particularly powerful in the medical transaction since health is fundamentally important to every aspect of life. As has been said:

> ...health designates the range of autonomy within which a person exercises control over his own biological state and over the conditions of his immediate environment. In this sense, health is identical with the degree of lived freedom.[4]

While orthodox medicine remains the main channel for health care, and the distributor of major resources in this respect, the extent of its control demands that it considers the wider social and political consequences, not only of the monopoly which it has over health care, but also of the manner in which this monopoly is used. These implications go beyond the narrow confines of techniques and technology and affect more than the medically defined health of the individual.

It has been said that 'Health and virtue are fundamental aspirations of human beings'.[5]   Perhaps for this reason, the World Health Organisation has claimed that there is a fundamental right to health.   This emphasis on health, when combined with the assumption that it is the practice of conventional medicine which will fulfil our desires for cure or at least for the alleviation of symptoms, places the doctor in a very powerful, but also very vulnerable, position. His power stems primarily from a monopoly over health services and the ability to control and manipulate the techniques and technology of medicine.   His vulnerability stems from the frustration of the expectations which claims of success help to raise in the patient who is striving to achieve or maintain health.

It is at the individual level that the relationship between man and medicine is at its most acute, and it is at this level that failures and grievances may become particularly important.   The expectations of, and dependence on, cure are at their strongest when the illess concerned is mine, and 'The culmination in a right and good healing action is what constitutes medicine qua medicine.'[6]   The clear implication that medicine has the potential for good, which presupposes the potential for evil as the absence of an anticipated good, has led some to claim that:

> Organised medicine has practically ceased to be the art of healing the curable, and consoling the hopeless has turned into a grotesque priesthood concerned with salvation and has become a law unto itself.[7]

To some extent the fundamental problem in contemporary medicine may relate as much as to the personal relationship between the patient and his doctor as it does to the competence of medicine as a discipline to fulfill the aspirations of the patient.   On the personal level the patient may well feel that 'the act of medical profession is inauthentic and a lie unless it fulfils that expectation of technical competence.'[8] These expectations of the patient may suggest that competence will include not simply the efficient application of therapy but also the accurate diagnosis of individual ills, and the manner in which the patient is handled.

However, although it has been suggested that the conflict with medicine may arise in fact out of the frustration of unreasonable expectations, it is a more complex and pervasive phenomenon than this would at first sight suggest. Medicine itself helps to create the expectations upon which it is subsequently judged by the patient. It is not merely the technical achievement of diagnosis, or the scientific promulgation of therapy, which may lead to generation of the hostility which may provoke the legal challenge. For, although the competent practice of medicine is important, its goal is also fundamental to the outcome of any transaction and that goal may vary with the individual's view of what it is to be healthy or 'cured'. So, it may be said that:

> competence is a necessary but not sufficient condition of a moral medical transaction and an authentic profession. Competence must itself be shaped by the end of the medical act - a right and good healing action for a particular patient.[9]

However, even at the level of technical capacity, despite the much vaunted advances of medicine and the increasing availability of therapies and 'cures', it is still possible for Illich to claim that 'The medical establishment has become a major threat to health'[10] and to continue that 'The pain, disability and anguish resulting from technical medical intervention now rival the morbidity due to traffic and industrial accidents...'[11] Claims of this sort reflect a more generalised dissatisfaction with medicine as a discipline as well as the personalised dissatisfaction, which might result more directly in the raising of an action when the individual returns from therapy to find himself no better off, or in some cases worse. Such dissatisfaction with the discipline of medicine may be a reflection of its failure to find cures for the most common ailments of mankind, while dissatisfaction at a personal level may relate not simply to the failure or lack of therapy, but also to the manner in which therapy is carried out. It is this second failure which relates to what has

been called the 'moral' aspect of medical practice and which requires
more than simple technical competence.

Thus, it is not simply negligence (as a legal concept) which
may generate the use of the negligence action. The patient may be as
much concerned with the wider concept of malpractice as with the
technical legal one of negligence. 'Malpractice', as the term is
used in the United Kingdom, can have wider implications than the use
of negligence terminology might imply and includes what Illich has
called 'Professional callousness, negligence and sheer
incompetence'.[12] The patient, feeling himself to be the victim of
any of these, rather than a willing and informed partner in a
fundamentally (to him at least) important transaction, may become
sufficiently disillusioned to seek recourse to the courts as a means
of airing the grievance and, hopefully, obtaining financial
compensation for his perceived loss or suffering.

The Legal Response

The role of the law, therefore, is fundamental in this area, since on
its definition of negligence, and its perception of the conflict, will
depend both the rights of the patient and the orientation of future
medical behaviour. Obviously, the wider the definition of negligence
which finds acceptance in the courts, the greater will be the legal
rights of the patient, and the more it resembles malpractice, the more
successfully will the patient who is disaffected raise an action.
The interpretation of what amounts to a well-founded, and therefore
potentially successful, action is dependent on the interpretation by
courts of the legal concept of negligence.

In order for the raising of an action to have any prospect of
success, it is necessary to show three things. First, that there was
a duty of care owed by one party (the party being sued) to another.
Second, that there was a breach of that duty of care, and third that
the harm which resulted stemmed from that breach of duty. These
rules apply in all cases of allegations of negligence, not simply
those which relate to medical practice. As has been said
'Essentially, in taking decisions of this sort, judges are applying
basic legal rules to a given set of facts',[13] and in so doing it

might be anticipated that consistency of the sort to which the law lays claim might emerge.

We have seen that the generation of the desire to use the negligence action may relate as much to the breakdown of the doctor/patient relationship as to the actual technical competence of the individual practitioner. The expectations which have been raised by medicine may make the use of this type of action more frequent where such breakdowns occur, even as standards of technical competence continue to increase. Such a breakdown might indeed result in harm to the patient (although the nature of the harm may be more psychological than physical), but does it make sense to talk of the doctor as having a duty to his patient to treat him well, and not simply competently? To put it another way, while the morality of medical practice may depend on just such factors, can the doctor's legal liability be framed also in these terms?

Doctors may have standards of professional practice to which they aspire and subscribe, but matters of professional behaviour are traditionally seen as internal to the profession, while those factors which relate to liability are generally acknowledged to be the legitimate interest of the law, whether or not this has the wholehearted approval of the profession itself. While it is generally agreed that all professions must be accountable to the community, and generally such accountability is ultimately achieved through the medium of the law, there is a certain reluctance on the part of the law to interfere with the practice of medicine. The law has developed in such a way as to limit the use of the negligence action and has shown a marked lack of interest in the way in which diagnoses are reached or information imparted to the patient.[14] Further, whether or not the patient may feel that he has a right to be treated in a certain manner, the law has left such matters as 'professional callousness' and the wider facets of malpractice to the medical profession itself.

We have already seen that the manner of dealing with the patient who claims that his or her full consent was not obtained depends on the interposing of criteria and factors which may relate rather to the perceived 'good' of medical practice, than to the proclaimed interests of the patient. This is no less the case with the traditional action of negligence, which expresses the harm which the consumer feels that medicine has done. Failure of personal relations in medicine, while acknowledged to be discomfiting and often unpleasant, is not seen as best resolved by the legal system. However, the importance of such factors as generators of the conflict which gives rise to the raising of an action should not be underestimated, and the raising of such actions, whether or not they are successful, has, as we shall see, important implications for medicine and its practitioners.

Central to decisions in cases of medical negligence is the undisputed fact that in all medical practice there is a risk. Even the most prudent or technically brilliant physician cannot guarantee absolute safety or success in the medical transaction. Thus, his liability has to be limited to those cases where the resultant harm was demonstrably due to his falling below the accepted level of care. This level, which is at the root of the negligence action, is set by the courts on the evidence of medical practitioners themselves. The evidence of physicians will therefore be highly influential in establishing the standards of expectation which are deemed to reflect the middle ground between the rights of the individual and the legally protected role of medicine. As Lord Denning has said:

> Medical science has conferred great benefits on mankind, but these benefits are attended by considerable risks....We cannot take the benefits without taking the risks.[15]

This statement, often repeated in decisions in this area, reflects several preconceptions which may stand in the way of the patient successfully raising an action.

First, there is the acceptance of medicine as a science, the implications being that it has essentially a clinical rather than a personal value. While the term 'medical science' is widely used, it is a misnomer of the practice of medicine insofar as it is dependent on trust and personal relationships for its success and not merely on technical scientific expertise, vide the fact that the administration by the doctor of a placebo may nonetheless so reassure the patient as to make him perceive himself as 'cured'.

Secondly, there is the acceptance of the great good which medicine has brought to the community. This claim is discussed elsewhere,[16] but it is one which has been fundamental in the shaping of all decisions on medical practice. Finally, there is the question of the risks which inevitably form part of the practice of medicine. Certainly, few would dispute that there is an attendant risk in the practice of medicine, and that once this risk is accepted it would be unreasonable to hold the doctor liable for the actual occurrence of that risk. However, as we have seen, not all risk will be disclosed, nor will courts demand disclosure to a high level. It therefore becomes unreasonable to use the inference that we are aware of risk to justify the risk not being the basis of a legal action, or at least of legitimate complaint. In no definition of consent does the acceptance of random risk play a part. For consent to be a defence to an allegation of negligence it is, however necessary that there is an acceptance of certain specific types of risk, and where this can be shown then the defence of volenti non fit injuria[17] will apply. As Walker has said[18]:

> If the plea is to succeed it must be shown not that the pursuer consented to take the risk of some harm befalling him, but that he consented to take the risk of the particular kind of harm which in fact befell him.[19]

Thus, the fact that the community may seem to accept that medical practice in general implies certain (random) risks, cannot logically be used against the individual who shows himself not to have accepted specific risks. While as a community in a general sense we may not take the benefits of medicine without also accepting its risks, this is an inappropriate logic to apply to the individual. Moreover, the fact that there is a high risk in medical practice would, according to the general rules of negligence, require the demonstration of a higher standard of care.[20] In medical cases, however, the belief in the value of medicine and its historical significance, has led to a balancing process whereby this general rule is modified. This raises the question of the public interest in the practice of medicine, and the issue of distribution of loss. Granted that the community has an interest in the success of the medical enterprise, this still provides no explicit reason why the individual who has been damaged by medicine should actually bear the loss. However, this is the inevitable outcome of this balancing process.

In any action in negligence against a medical practitioner, the law has accepted, apparently unquestioningly, the 'good' of health, and will often refer to the community interests as a basis for not finding a doctor negligent even where there is a clearly established duty and it is clear that the harm complained of resulted from the intervention of medicine. This may serve to contribute to the increased burden of proof which the pursuer may feel he has to carry in allegations of this sort.

There are few problems, however, in establishing at least some parts of the requirements for the raising of an action in negligence against a doctor. While some discussion in the past centred on the problems of establishing the duty required by law, it is now clear that the offer to treat is sufficient to create the legal duty whose breach may result in an action being raised. It is however, in the latter two constituent elements of the requirements of establishing negligence that problems may arise. The evaluation of what is a duty will take logical precedence over the question of breach, and in assessing the nature and extent of the doctor's duties to his patients, the law will have recourse to consideration of a number of differing factors. These considerations may affect the final decisions about duties taken in a court of law, and will certainly reflect on the extent to which the practice of medicine can legally be challenged.

Despite what may commonly be thought, the duties of the doctor do not include making an accurate diagnosis,[21] nor do they necessarily require him to follow established methods of therapy.[22] Indeed, there are some difficulties in establishing what duties are actually owed to a patient by a doctor, at least in specific terms. The general duty would seem to be defined as acting with 'due skill and care', but the essential constituents of 'due skill and care' are less than clear. Further, there are considerable problems in assessing what amounts to a legal duty of care where the practice under consideration is that of the doctor. In the assessment of what amounts to a legal duty there is the additional problem that the doctor's choices as to diagnosis and therapy are expressly protected. The use of this 'clinical judgment' is jealously guarded by medicine, and is given as a prime reason for minimising the impact of law on medicine and the level of accountability which is possible.

The doctor's duties to his patient, then, are rather vague, but centre primarily on his behaving with the skill and care which can be expected of another doctor at the same level of competence in the same circumstances. The assessment of his behaviour will depend to a large extent on the nature of the evidence of other practitioners as to what their behaviour would have been in the same circumstances. In all cases of alleged negligence, it is of course true that the evidence of fellow professionals will weigh heavily with courts.

Up to a certain point professional evidence is of course vital. However, to use this information as the exclusive indicator of the nature and extent of a duty is to equate professional practice with the description of a legal duty. The existence and definition of a legal duty, which may of course include a reflection of what professionals actually do or will excuse, are matters which are for legal rather than professional delimitation. Indeed, it is in the assessment of the reasonableness of any number of professional practices that the civil law finds its essential role. While the information to be assessed may well be technical, the role of the law goes beyond the narrow confines of professional practice and relates to wider and more fundamental considerations such as the standards which are acceptable to the community. Were it otherwise, then the law could serve only a minimal function in the assessment of many cases of alleged liability for negligence, and the decision makers would exclusively be fellow professionals whose disinterest cannot be guaranteed. Our legal system, indeed, is designed to ensure that decisions of this sort are taken by disinterested (albeit non-technical) adjudicators, rather than by expert (but not necessarily disinterested) specialists. To do otherwise is to usurp one of the major roles of the law in our society.

There is however one area where the role of the professional witness may be of paramount assistance to the courts and that is where the basis of the alleged negligence is a deviation from 'normal practice'. Where this forms the basis of the allegations, it is necessary to establish several things:- first, that there was a usual or normal practice; second that there was a deviation from that practice; and third that the deviation was such that no doctor acting with due skill and care would have made.[23] Clearly the first of these will depend heavily on the evidence of fellow professionals.

Indeed, it is difficult to see how the existence or not of a standard practice could otherwise be established. The most important of these criteria is the last which must also depend on the opinion of other professionals, but if the law is to perform its role adequately, it cannot depend exclusively on this evidence.

If the court rather than the expert witness is to be the ultimate decision-maker then there must be room for interpretation and analysis of the information provided. In criminal cases, the evidence even of a number of experts need not be accepted by the court should it wish to draw alternative conclusions. This ability to make choices independently of expert advice, is one which also extends to the civil law. Indeed, almost by definition, the court in assessing allegations of negligence will be confronted with conflicting experts, whose opinions will be interpreted and used according the court's attitude to the case. When dealing with medical negligence cases, this is particularly so. Medical schools, for example, are expressly prohibited from teaching only one aspect of medicine or one particular school of medical thought, and inevitably different practices will arise out of this. Equally the influence of the hierarchy in local situations may serve to dictate that practices will vary from area to area. It is likely then that both the pursuer and the defender in any case will be able to back up their assertions with competing claims of experts in medicine, making the court's role as adjudicator more vital than ever. No question of credibility is likely to arise either, since the likelihood is that both sets of opposing witnesses will be eminent and disinterested parties.

The role of the court, in allegations of medical negligence as in all other cases, will be its traditional one of sifting the evidence and plumping for the most 'just' and practicable verdict. Samples of medical negligence cases, however, would tend to suggest that courts have been more likely, on policy rather than credibility terms, to favour the evidence given by the doctor's (defender's) witnesses. Perhaps this is less than surprising given that it must cast some doubt on the claims of the pursuer, but it should also be remembered that the claimant only has to prove his allegations on the civil standard of proof, the balance of probabilitites, and not on the criminal standard of beyond reasonable doubt.

Deciding what amounts to a breach of the duty of care will

therefore raise considerable problems. Given that the nature of the duties owed is somewhat vague, there are few guidelines to indicate what amounts to breach, and again this will depend heavily on the information provided by other doctors. Since the establishing of the duty between doctor and patient is relatively straightforward, much will hinge on the interpretation of whether or not a specific duty exists to do X, and on the subsequent question of whether or not that specific duty has been breached. It is clear from decisions made by courts in the past that it is not a simple matter to estimate this as a prospective litigant. The recent case of Whitehouse v. Jordan[24] demonstrated clearly what kinds of problems may face the pursuer even on a strict legal interpretation. The Court of Appeal[25] clearly wanted to say that where a doctor makes an error of judgment, this does not amount to negligence, and while the House of Lords modified this view by rephrasing it in terms that an error of judgment will not always amount to negligence, logically, since doctors are not required, for example, to make accurate diagnosis, it will be likely that an error of judgment will seldom be held to amount to negligence in law.

Further, before such interpretation and application of legal rules takes place, there are a number of factors and variables which must be taken into account as they may be fundamentally important, consciously or sub-consciously, to the decision-makers. In interpreting what is a breach of duty, the law takes into account considerations which are not simply concerned with the behaviour of the particular doctor in relation to the particular patient, but rather to the perceived interests and well-being of the community, or the medical profession, as a whole. Lord Denning, for example, has claimed, 'we should be doing a disservice to the community at large if we were to impose liability on hospitals and doctors for everything that happens to go wrong...'[26] This is again based on the notion that the element of risk which exists in every medical transaction will modify rather than increase the duty of care, and is a further example of the problems in distributing loss. Here again it would seem that it is the individual rather then the community who must bear the loss. It also, however, reflects the difference between medical negligence and medical mishap or accident. While liability will arise in respect of the former, it will not arise in respect of the

latter.   But it also assumes that the interests of the medical
profession and those of the community always correspond, which is an
assumption which cannot readily be justified.   Indeed, the nature of
the risk factor in medicine, which is used as an excusing condition
here, is generally though to raise rather than lower the standard of
care which is demanded by law.

Taking into consideration the bias of the law towards the
protection of medicine as a general good, it is hardly surprising that
it has not tended to view the wider concept of malpractice as being
actionable, but has narrowed the boundaries of what amounts to
negligence in legal terms.   The incompetent practice of medicine is
thus the central feature of the negligence action.

Leaving aside the problems of this narrow approach, it is clear
that the general tests of the negligence action are not as
consistently applied in medical cases as might be expected given that
no overt differentiation in favour of medicine is said to take
place.   Now, what amounts to competent medical practice is open to
interpretation and may reflect the same bias as does the
interpretation of other factors, but there is often a marked
divergence between the lay and the legal conception of medical
negligence.   The patient may perceive competence as including those
skills which the doctor professes to have and which form the very
essentials of the patient's decision to consult the doctor and, where
applicable, to accept therapy.   Thus, the patient may regard an
accurate diagnosis as fundamental evidence of competence, particularly
since, as we have seen, medicine as a whole lays claim to a monopoly
in the area of health.   The law will not.   The patient may regard
the wisdom of the doctor's choice of action as being subject to
scientific and calculable rules, whereas the law will not, depending
rather on the latitude offered by the use of 'clinical judgment'.

As we have seen, in order to support such interpretation, the
law uses not only the perceived value of medicine as a discipline, but
also applies the concept of the 'reasonable' doctor by reference to
standards of practice.   Thus there is an averaging out of the
characteristics of any one medical transaction into the expectations
which fellow professionals may have of the doctor in question and of
themselves, in the same way as the law will judge the ordinary citizen
according to the test of the 'reasonable man'.   This man does not, of

course, exist. He is merely a device to judge behaviour by, and is 'presumed to be free both from over-apprehension and from over-confidence'.[27] To that extent it might seem that he can be routinely identified as the balanced paradigm of rationality, recognised by the application of objective tests in any given case. However, as Lord Macmillan has pointed out:

> there is a sense in which the standard of care of the reasonable man involves in its application a subjective element. It is still left to the judge to decide what, in the circumstances of the particular case, the reasonable man would have had in contemplation, and what, accordingly, the party sought to be made liable ought to have foreseen. Here there is room for diversity of view....[28]

The interpretation of what amounts to the reasonable skill and care will be subject to just such subjective elements which will by definition reflect the attitudes of the decision-makers both to the individual doctor, and to the beneficial nature of medicine as a whole. The esteem in which medicine is held also provides a particular place in these decisions for the professional colleagues of the person whose competence is being challenged, and it is not unreasonable to suggest that their instinct will be to defend rather than to criticise their colleague.

In demonstrating apparent reluctance to hold a doctor legally liable for the consequences of his actions the courts therefore provide a reinforcement of medical mythology. Not only is the discipline as a whole seen as worthy of protection, even despite the propensity for harm which we have already discussed, but the individual practitioner as representative of the profession and the discipline is seen as meriting special treatment, even to the point of protecting his career and prospects.

It is noteworthy that on the one hand, the law serves to reinforce what Kennedy[29] has called the 'engineer - scientist' image of the doctor, and on the other hand claims that scientific certainty is inimical to the practice of medicine. Equally, the failure of the 'engineer/scientist' to take the correct decision is protected by the claim that 'an error of judgment is not necessarily negligence'. It would seem to have become a corollary of the advances in medical treatment to which this model of medicine aspires and of the monopoly which conventional medicine has over diagnosis and treatment, that the doctor's choice of therapy and technique are seen as being incapable of judgment by those outwith the profession itself. While the courts may occasionally be prepared to hold that a particular procedure was negligently carried out, they are extremely unlikely to comment on or interfere with the choice of diagnostic technique or therapy or even to examine the expected benefits of such choices. This protection of the 'clinical judgment' of the doctor may serve to protect the practitioners of medicine, but fails to recognise that it may be precisely the exercise of this judgment which provides the fuel for the doctor/patient confrontation.

Defensive Medicine

The Royal Commission on Civil Liability and Compensation for Personal Injury (Pearson Commission)[30] found that while successful claims are achieved in about 80% of all personal injury cases, the average rate in medical claims is only about 30-40%. This is not, however, entirely based on any apparent reluctance to find doctors negligent, but may more reflect extra-legal intervention in the settlement of claims. The intervention of the medical Defence Unions,[31] which filter out the more clear cut cases of negligence, may paradoxically result in only those doctors whose behaviour is viewed as defensible, after legal and medical advice, actually being sued in a court of law. This undoubted fact must to some extent explain the shortfall in successful actions, but it is by no means the sole explanation.

It has been suggested that courts take account of factors other than purely legal ones in their assessment of medical negligence cases, and this may serve to explain the apparent preference for the evidence of the defence specialist. Where this attitude is adopted it is justified by pointing to a number of considerations, particularly the experience in the United States of America where 'defensive medicine' would seem to be on the increase, and this increase is perceived as partly the result of the willingness of juries to find against a doctor in negligence cases. Defensive medicine is variously defined as optimal medicine or, more commonly, as the unnecessary use of diagnostic and treatment measures in an effort to avoid possible legal action. While the dangers of defensive medicine are real, particularly in as much as they involve the patient in more technical medical intervention, the logical outcome of finding the negligent doctor to be negligent is not necessarily the practice of this sort of medicine.

Moreover, the reluctance of courts to compensate the victims of medicine may itself produce the impetus to threaten or challenge medicine further, by creating the atmosphere of hostility which is a likely outcome of poor success rates against a specific professional group. As was said earlier, whether or not the outcome of the case is that the patient 'wins', the raising of increasing numbers of actions is of importance to the practice of medicine, and may also be likely to contribute to the defensive response from doctors which may place patients at even greater risk.

In fact, the fear of 'defensive' medicine does not stand up well to close scrutiny. Some, indeed, would claim that 'defensive' medicine is merely optimal medicine. While this may be going too far, there is little doubt that 'defensive medicine' has a higher chance of resulting in accurate diagnosis and thereby of equating more closely with the expectations of the patient, whatever the standards set by medicine or the law. In any event, there are good reasons for suggesting that the practice of this type of highly invasive medicine is not the logical outcome of an increased success rate in negligence actions. 'Defensive' medicine has arisen primarily in the United States as a result of the so-called 'negligence explosion'. The impact of this has been a huge increase in the raising of actions against doctors and a corresponding rise in success rates in these actions.

This change in pattern is not however necessarily the result of poor medical practice. Many of the factors which have contributed to the rising number of actions against doctors can be seen to relate to what has been called here 'malpractice' rather than necessarily to a falling in standards of technical competence. It has been said, for example, that the private structure of health services, the real or imagined wealth of the doctor and the increasing emphasis on the scientific nature of medicine have combined to reduce the personal, sympathetic relationship between doctor and patient which offered some protection to the doctor. However, other factors leading to the 'negligence explosion' are, however, equally unlikely to occur in the United Kingdom.

First, there is the practice of lawyers in charging contingency fees, which means that, where a case is successful, the lawyer will receive reimbursement to the tune of a percentage of the award made. This, it is claimed, leads more lawyers to accept and initiate cases of this sort. While there must be a limitation on this, since where there is no award no fees are charged, there is little doubt that it will contribute to the raising of actions which are not certain of success.

Further, where this occurs, the practice of juries assessing both negligence and the level of awards is said to increase the likelihood of a successful action and to raise the level of damages, with the anticipated results on medical practice. Finally, the fact that medicine is a private enterprise in the United States, coupled with the fact that Americans seem to be more litigious than the British, more readily using courts to settle claims which the British might regard as social or political rather than purely legal, have also contributed their measure to the development of 'defensive medicine'. This practice is thus unlikely to occur on a large scale, for these reasons at least, in the United Kingdom.

There are, however, further implications of the defensive medicine argument which require to be appraised. Can we really accept that the negligent doctor being found negligent will influence substantially the behaviour of his non-negligent colleagues? Or, if it does, can we expect that the influence which this might have will necessarily be for the worse? It may be that there is some kick-back effect, but it is unclear why this should not be a raising of standards accompanying an increased awareness of public accountability, rather than the institution of unnecessary or over-zealous medical intervention.

A further factor which seems to have influenced at least some judges has been the status which the doctor may claim in the community. This is particularly interesting since it is not clear why the lorry driver or the architect should not equally lay claim to a certain status. Nonetheless, they are offered no special status at law. The use of this criterion is also of interest since it has served to provide the courts, at least in some cases, with a further justification for tinkering with the clear rules of the law in medical cases. Some judges have shown themselves to be particularly concerned with this aspect of decision-making, claiming that the doctor's status affects the nature of the proof which may be required to establish negligence. Thus, Lord Denning for example, claimed in one case at least that the doctor's position in the community makes the allegation of negligence more serious and correspondingly raises the burden of proof.[32] This is further evidence of the weight attached to the doctor at least by courts of law, and, while not always so overtly expressed, may in fact form the basis of the attitudes which have been identified as being likely to make the proof of negligence in these cases more problematic.

Conclusion

There can be little doubt in general terms that the role of the law is fundamental to the protection of the individual. It may then seem to be paradoxical that the dissatisfaction of the 'consumer' with the product is not taken as the starting point for decision-making but is apparently seen as the unfortunate but unavoidable result of a discipline whose benefits are clear and unchallengeable, and whose innate risks are particularly high. The credulity of the law and the community to the claims of medical practice is such that effective controls seem to be lacking.

Primarily, the individual has the mechanism of the law by which to register his dissatisfaction and distress and to receive compensation for damage done. And yet, while the morality of medicine goes largely unconsidered and the aims of the discipline unchallenged, the law is likely to prove an ineffective means of providing effective control of medicine. On the contrary, the intervention of the law may lead to a rationalising exercise which does not reinforce optimal procedures or standards, and which is in any event circumscribed by the prejudices of its decision-makers which become sanctified by the dependence of the law on precedent. While the law may legitimately claim to represent and safeguard the interests of the individual and through him the welfare of the community, there is in this area an apparent failure to distinguish the good of good medical treatment from the vested interests of the practitioners of medicine. As Illich says:

> The medical clergy can be controlled only if the law is used to restrict and disestablish its monopoly on deciding what constitutes disease, who is sick, and what ought to be done to him or her.[33]

As it is, the interests of the individual claimant are subjugated to the perceived good of the group, a classic utilitarian move.

However, although the utilitarian ethical principle may at first sight justify this attitude, it is evident that an essential component of such claims is that there is a maximisation of benefit to the community from the subjugation of such interests. Many would claim that there is little evidence for this, and certainly no grounds for belief that the interests of the community are in fact well served by the discarding of the rights of these individuals or groups.

Instead of the attitude of the individual consumer being taken as a reflection of the type of expectations of medical practice to which the courts as representatives of the community might aspire, it is the hostility of the medical profession to interference in its practice which would seem to be the starting point.[34] Some kind of balance must be achieved. The doctor must be free to practice as he chooses and cannot do so efficiently, we are told, when the 'dagger' of the negligence action points at his back. Certainly we must be guided by the attitudes of the doctor's professional colleagues in assessing his behaviour and if his colleagues would not have criticised his behaviour, then the law must take this into account. On the other hand the individual patient must have an effective recourse against medical incompetence. Determining the issue exclusively by recourse to the judgment of the medical profession itself can only be a sure method of decision-making where the faith of the community in the discipline is such that it makes an actual choice to do this. It is not clear that this has occurred in the case of conventional medicine. Moreover, as we have seen, the practice of the discipline is not truly scientific for it includes the personal variables and fallibilities which medicine uses as its excuses for apparently incompetent practice.

The claim by the medical profession that 'negligence is a legal and not a medical concept'[35] and that doctors should therefore be more concerned at the disapprobation of their colleagues than that of the law, shows both the desires of the profession for a monopoly over decision-making and also its disapproval of the (albeit limited) incursions of the law into the practice of medicine, and into the control which doctors have over the content, ethics and practice of medicine. This indeed is a medicine which is 'defensive'. The inability or unwillingness of the law to make greater inroads into the control of a fundamentally important community resource, and one which has many deep and important implications for all, means that the responsibility for ensuring that the conflict between doctor and patient does not occur is placed firmly on the medical profession itself whose vested interests may not equate with those of the recipient or patient.

However, doctors may claim, and indeed sometimes do, that the greatest threat to medical practice and therefore a main problem for the well-being of the community, is precisely that the law may interfere in decisions which are essentially medical. Of necessity, legal assessment of medical practice is inexpert and incomplete and it is certainly clear that problems arise both in interpretation of the jargon of the discipline (as with other disciplines also) and in the assessment of what amounts to a reasonable or good medical action. While acknowledging the limitations of medicine, and the fallibility of its practitioners, few would seek or endorse a radical intervention from the law in this area unless circumstances justified it.

Nonetheless, if the nature of the medical enterprise is indeed to be a morally justifiable one, then its goals and methods cannot simply be defined by the group of professionals, whose aims in any event may be unclear. The main function of the law in this area cannot be exclusively to support the views of one group over those of another, nor is it practicable, desirable or even necessary to view all medical decisions with the type of suspicion which may be argued for by some. The law serves its purpose by balancing, in this area as in others, what might be seen as the policy views of the community, the interests of professional grouos and the wellbeing and rights of the individual. The professionalism of medicine should not and does not imply that it is unaccountable, but neither should the personal frustrations of the patient inevitably lead to a successful action against the doctor. The doctor is indeed 'responsible for the scientific, medical, legal and moral implications of his decisions'.[36]   This liability is however dramatically reduced where the standards set by the law amount to the lowest common denominator rather than to the optimal standard of health care which it is reasonable for the patient to expect.   The doctor, in committing himself to the ethic of Hippocrates, pledges his first loyalty to his patient, not to the scientific enterprise of medicine.   This involves a wider understanding of the idea of professional negligence than that which is tied up in the existing legal definition.   It means the adoption of standards which equate more closely to the use of the term malpractice outlined here.

The engineer/scientist model must not be permitted to predominate the practice of medicine.   The inevitable outcome of this is increasing disaffection, more intervention and increasing pressure on courts to interfere in ways which may not always be helpful.   The morality of medicine must always be found in its striving for the right treatment for the particular patient.   The law will aggregate and rationalise, but the ethical practice of medicine is highly personalised and therefore highly volatile.

When both the law and medical practice can less defensively accept the fallibility of medicine and its practitioners, the impetus for vexatious litigation will be reduced, and standards of medical practice will be pitched more reasonably than the overly high expectations of many patients, or the overly basic ones of the law. The 'technician applying scientific rules to classes of patients'[37] is the more likely victim of the negligence action, and his patient the more likely victim of the unacceptable face of modern technology and medicine.   The development of the medical profession towards becoming a group in which the patient may rationally place his trust is the first major step in the avoidance of 'defensive' medicine and the so-called negligence explosion.   It is the breakdown in this trust, which may be the result of the de-personalising of medicine as well as of its fight for control of health, which characterises the typical breeding ground for the conflict between doctor and patient.

NOTES

1. Pellegrino, E., and Thomasma, D., <u>A Philosophical Basis of Medical Practice</u>, O.U.P., 1981, at p. 66.
2. Pellegrino and Thomasma, op.cit., at p. 125.
3. ibid., at p. ix.
4. Illich, I., <u>Limits to Medicine. Medical Nemesis: The Expropriation of Health</u>, Harmondsworth, Penguin Books, 1977 edition, at p. 244.
5. Pellegrino and Thomasma, op.cit., at p. vii.
6. ibid., at p. 211.
7. Illich, op.cit., at p. 249.
8. Pellegrino and Thomasma, op.cit., at p. 213.
9. id.
10. Illich, op.cit., at p. 11.
11. op.cit., at p. 35.
12. op.cit., at p. 38.
13. McLean, S.A.M., 'Negligence – A Dagger at the Doctor's Back?' in Robson, P., and Watchman, P., (eds), <u>Justice, Lord Denning and the Constitution</u>, Aldershot, Gower Publishing Co., 1981, 99, at p. 100.
14. For further discussion, see chapters 5 supra and 9 infra.
15. <u>Roe</u> v. <u>Minister of Health</u> [1954] 2 Q.B. 66, at p. 83.
16. See chapter 10, infra.
17. Broadly, this defence is based on the principle that where a person voluntarily assumes a risk, he cannot then recover from the other party to the agreement when that risk actually occurs. For further discussion, see Watson, A.A., and McLean, A.M., 'Consent to Treatment – A Shield or a Sword' 25 <u>Scott. Med. J.</u> (1980) 113.
18. Walker, D.M., <u>The Law of Delict in Scotland</u>, Edinburgh, W. Green & Son, 1966.
19. ibid., at pp. 351-2.
20. See <u>Glasgow Corporation</u> v. <u>Muir</u> [1943] A.C. 448.
21. <u>Whiteford</u> v. <u>Hunter and Gleed</u> The Lancet (1948) Vol. 2, 232; (1949) Vol. 1, 586; (1950) Vol. 2, 643.
22. <u>Hunter</u> v. <u>Hanley</u> 1955 S.C. 200.
23. <u>Hunter</u> v. <u>Hanley</u>, supra cit.
24. [1981] 1 All E.R. 267 (H.L.).

25. [1980] 1 All E.R. 650.

26. Roe v. Minister of Health, supra cit., at p. 86.

27. Glasgow Corporation v. Muir, supra cit., at p. 457.

28. id.

29. Kennedy, I., The Unmasking of Medicine, London, George Allen & Unwin, 1981.

30. Cmnd 7054/1978.

31. These are organisations which all doctors are advised to join, and which offer both legal advice and also, where appropriate, may settle a case of alleged negligence or offer a defence for the doctor in a court of law.

32. Hucks v. Cole 'The Times' 9 May 1968.

33. op.cit., at p. 251.

34. See Lord Denning in Hatcher v. Black 'The Times' 2 July 1954.

35. Leahy Taylor, J., The Doctor and Negligence, Pitman Medical, 1971, at p. 1.

36. Pellegrino and Thomasma, op.cit., at p. x.

37. Illich, op.cit., at pp. 38-9.

9 Confidentiality

The importance of the idea of confidentiality for the study of medical practice lies in the fact that it illustrates several features of the social role of medicine, including the central one that the doctor-patient relationship is itself a social relationship which involves a number of moral and legal rights and duties. But it should be said at once that although it is generally assumed that confidentiality plays a direct and important role in medicine, the nature of the concept of confidentiality is not clear. In this chapter, we shall attempt to clarify the idea of confidentiality in medical practice in order to bring out the different and competing values that are reflected in it. At the same time, we shall seek to give some substance to the general notion of confidentiality by looking at ways in which law and medicine interact in this area.

Confidentiality is deeply rooted in the tradition of medical practice (though the view has been put that there is no continuity to this tradition[1]). Thus the Hippocratic Oath contains the vow:

> Whatever in connection with my professional practice, or not in connection with it, I see or hear, in the life of men which ought not to be spoken of abroad, I will not divulge as reckoning that all such should be kept secret.

The recent Handbook of Medical Ethics issued by the British Medical Association contains a number of references to professional confidence, the most pertinent of which are as follows:[2]

> 1.5 The nature of professional confidence varies according to the form of consultation or examination but

in each of the three forms of relationship the doctor is responsible to the patient or person with whom he is in a professional relationship for the security and confidentiality of information given to him.

1.6 A doctor must preserve secrecy on all he knows.

There are five exceptions to this general principle

(1) The patient gives consent
(2) When it is undesirable on medical grounds to seek a patient's consent.
(3) The doctor's overriding duty to society
(4) For the purpose of medical research, approved by the Chairman of the BMA's Central Ethical Committee or his nominee
(5) The information is required by due legal process.

1.7 A doctor must be able to justify his decision to disclose information.

A number of writers have made the point that the width of the exceptions to the general principle is such as to render the principle of confidentiality as almost meaningless.   What, for example, is the range of the doctor's overriding duty to society and how extensive is the discretion given to the doctor to decide that medical grounds exist for not seeking the patient's consent to disclosure?   Take for example the exception that the information is required by due legal process.   One implication of this exception is that the doctor has no 'testimonial privilege', i.e., he cannot refuse to give evidence to a court of law on the ground that he would breach confidence in so doing.[3]   Indeed the law at times gives the doctor a positive duty to make known information derived from the doctor-patient relationship.   Thus it is a criminal offence for a doctor not to notify the district medical officer of health that he has attended on a patient suffering from a so-called notifiable disease, which category includes cholera, plague, relapsing fever, smallpox, and typhus.[4]

There are also occasions when doctors are under a duty to provide information concerning criminal conduct and this duty is held to apply even if the doctor learns of the criminal conduct through the doctor-patient relationship.   For example, the Prevention of Terrorism (Temporary Provisions) Act 1976, section 11 makes it an offence for any person not to disclose to the police any information

174

which might be of material assistance in preventing an act of terrorism or in securing the arrest of any person involved in terrorist activity. Similarly the Road Traffic Act 1972, section 168 makes it an offence to fail to give information leading to the identification of drivers alleged to have committed various offences under the Act.

In the case of Hunter v. Mann,[5] a doctor had treated two people who had been injured in a car accident. The doctor advised both patients to visit the police concerning the matter but they did not do so. Later the doctor was approached by the police who sought information about the identity of a person suspected of having committed the offence of dangerous driving. The doctor refused to give the names of the two parties whom he had treated on the ground that the information was confidential because it had been obtained through the relationship of doctor and patient, and he had not obtained their consent to disclose their identities to the police. The doctor was later charged with an offence under section 168 of the Act and was convicted. The court refused to recognise that the confidential relationship between doctor and patient afforded the doctor any defence in the present case. It was noted in court that the statement of professional ethics issued by the BMA itself makes an exception to the general rule of confidentiality where information is required by law. Further, the law puts a duty to provide the relevant information on 'any person' with such information, and doctors were within this category. However, it was noted that the doctor was placed in a difficult position:

> May I say, before leaving the case, that I appreciate the concern of a responsible medical practitioner who feels that he is faced with a conflict of duty. That the defendant was conscious of a conflict and realised his duty both to society and to his patient is clear from the finding of the justices, but he may find comfort, although the decision goes against him, from the following. First, that he has only to disclose information which may lead to identification and not other confidential matters; secondly, that the result, in my judgment, is entirely consistent with the rules that the British Medical Association have laid down.[6]

This passage is of interest for it illustrates one of the features about the general principle of confidentiality which was noted earlier, namely that both the statement of the principle and the exceptions to it are so broad that the principle is either vacuous or useless as a guide to practical reasoning. Clearly there is a conflict of duty where the law forces doctors to do something (such as giving information) which would not be allowed by the principle of confidentiality. But to reason, as does the statement of the general principle, that the duty laid down by the law always has precedence is in effect to give no weight to the idea of confidentiality, and does not really recognise the conflict of duty as a real, rather than an apparent, one.

Indeed one writer has dismissed the idea of confidentiality as nothing more than pious rhetoric.[7] However it may well be that the difficulty lies in the very conception of confidentiality used in discussions of the issue, for it appears that if it is an idea central to medical practice (which it is commonly taken to be), then it may require reformulation.

One immediate difficulty is that it is not apparent how a relationship which involves confidence can by itself generate a principle with moral weight. Clearly as a practical measure medicine requires a background whereby patients do not feel inhibited in what they tell doctors. Indeed in some areas of medicine, especially psychiatric medicine, treatment would be impossible if this were not so. And it may indeed be the case that patients would not speak openly and frankly to doctors if they thought that what they said would be passed on to other people. But this consideration is purely a practical one, about the viability of medicine and of the doctor-patient relationship, and in itself hardly gives any moral weight to a principle of confidentiality.

Rather, it will be argued, there are two distinct ways of taking the principle of confidentiality; furthermore, the statement of the principle usually adopted fails to make clear which of these senses is directly used, with the result, already noted, that the principle appears either vacuous or meaningless. The two modes of understanding confidentiality can be appreciated in terms of the difference in perspective of the two sides of the doctor-patient relationship.

1. First, there is the perspective of the patient. His concern

with confidentiality is that his involvement with a doctor to some extent threatens his autonomy in that he divulges information about himself. In other words, the moral basis for confidentiality viewed from this perspective is the patient's right to privacy. Although the right to privacy is only somewhat non-systematically recognised by law (and in the United Kingdom as opposed to America there is no explicit legal right as such), in terms of moral argument the idea of privacy has been of value in explaining aspects of the moral nature of personal autonomy. Central to this is the idea that every person has the right as a moral agent to determine his own life, and this includes choices about making known facts about himself, especially where these facts are relevant to his perception of his own identity and self-esteem. A further point is that the principle of confidentiality is simply a consequence of the place of consent in medical practice. If the moral autonomy of the patient is to be respected, then the patient must consent to all aspects of it, including the divulgence or withholding of information concerning himself.

2. A quite different view of confidentiality can be arrived at by considering what might be called the doctor's perspective. Here the central concern is with the judgments and decisions which the doctor must make as part of his role as a medical expert. Since the doctor is treated as the expert in the field of medicine, certain matters are for him alone to know, and are not the proper concern of anyone else. The basic value underlying confidentiality as viewed from this perspective is that of the professional autonomy of the doctor. If doctors were required to divulge all information derived from relationships with their patients, then such autonomy would be threatened, and doctors would find their freedom of clinical judgement to be in danger, perhaps to the extent that medical decisions could no longer be made.

It is obvious that there is quite a radical difference in the idea and function of confidentiality as viewed from the perspectives of the patient and of the doctor. This difference can be appreciated in terms of the two broad approaches to moral theory which we identified in chapter 1, namely autonomy-based ethics and

utilitarianism.   The patient's perspective on confidentiality derives
support from the first of these two general theories, which emphasises
the idea of respect for persons as moral ends in themselves.   The
central role of the rights of the patient to knowledge about his
medical condition and treatment also coheres with the importance of
taking rights seriously which is a focal point of autonomy-based
ethics.   In contrast, the doctor's perspective on confidentiality is
more suited to utilitarian philosophy, for it adopts the position that
the rights of the patient are to be subordinated to the efficient
operation of medicine, an aim which confidentiality promotes.   On
this view, confidentiality has no inherent value, as autonomy theories
would argue;   rather, its value is that it is a precondition of the
existence of the general institution of medicine, which is a social
benefit to be valued accordingly.

The difference in perspective on confidentiality also parallels
to some extent a difference in the idea of the doctor-patient
relationship, which can be taken as either a purely technical or
advisory matter in which the doctor is the agent of the patient whose
consent is crucial to the whole relationship, or alternatively the
relationship is seen as one involving definite and fixed aims (mainly
those relating to the cure or restoration of health of the patient)
and the central aspect is the mode in which the doctor acts to achieve
these aims.[8]   However, we should note that the general principle of
confidentiality embodies aspects of both the patient's and the
doctor's perspectives, a feature which no doubt partially explains the
difficulty which is felt in explaining the general principle in a
coherent way.

The ambiguity of perspective of the principle of
confidentiality can well be illustrated by considering some features
of the law on the subject.   Two legal topics in particular are
instructive on this score.

1.   Testimonial privilege.   It was noted earlier that doctors do not
possess any right to refuse to give evidence on the ground that the
evidence in question derived from the doctor-patient relationship.
For example in the case of Nuttall v. Nuttall & Twyman,[9] in an
action for divorce on the ground of adultery, the defendant's
psychiatrist was cited as a witness by the plaintiff.   The

psychiatrist expressed extreme reluctance to testify, pointing out that confidence played a special role in the relationship between patient and psychiatrist as patients believed what they said would remain secret. Despite this argument, the court ruled that the psychiatrist would be in contempt of court if he persisted in his refusal, and in the end he gave the evidence required.

It should be noted however that although the formal position is that doctors do not enjoy testimonial privilege, in practice the courts will take steps to respect the doctor's confidentiality. The classic statement of this position is to be found in the case of Attorney General v. Mulholland; Foster,[10] where Lord Denning M.R. said:

> The only profession that I know which is given a privilege from disclosing information to a court of law is the legal profession and then it is not the privilege of the lawyer but of his client. Take the clergyman, the banker or the medical man. None of these is entitled to refuse to answer when directed to by a judge. Let me not be mistaken. The judge will respect the confidences which each member of these honourable professions receives in the course of it, and will not direct him to answer unless not only it is relevant but also it is a proper and, indeed, necessary question in the course of justice to be put and answered. A judge is the person entrusted, on behalf of the community, to weigh these conflicting interests - to weigh on the one hand the respect due to confidence in the profession and on the other hand, the ultimate interest of the community in justice being done.

Similarly in Hunter v. Mann [11] it was observed by Lord Widgery C.J.:

> ...if a doctor, giving evidence in court, is asked a question which he finds embarrassing because it involves him talking about things which he would normally regard as confidential, he can seek the protection of the judge and ask the judge if it is necessary for him to answer. The judge, by virtue of the overriding discretion to control his court which all English judges have, can, if he thinks fit, tell the doctor that he need not answer the question. Whether or not the judge would take that line, of course, depends largely on the importance of the potential answer to the issues being tried.

Several points should be noted about the idea of privilege not to testify and the refusal by the law to extend this privilege beyond the legal profession itself. The first and crucial one is that the privilege belongs to the patient or client rather than to the doctor or other professional. Thus in Schneider v. Leigh,[12] a doctor was asked to prepare a medical report on behalf of defendants who were being sued for damages for personal injuries. Extracts of the report were later shown to the plaintiff in the action who took the view that the report was defamatory and raised a separate action for libel against the doctor. The court held that the doctor enjoyed no claim to privilege as regards the libel action. It was pointed out that the privilege belonged to the company who were the defendants in the personal injuries action but to no-one else. Indeed the company could if it wished waive its privilege without the consent of the doctor.

Schneider v. Leigh also illustrates a further point about the rules on privilege of witnesses. This is that the law gives an overriding importance to the idea of litigation as a means of resolving disputes and the extent and limits of privilege can be understood only in terms of this policy. Of course, for the law to take this view is an example of the value placed on the professional autonomy of the legal profession itself, for the result is that the only profession which does have such a privilege is that of the law. Thus Hodson L.J. said in Schneider v. Leigh,[13] 'It is essential to bear in mind that the privilege is the privilege of the litigant, accorded to him in order that he may be protected in preparing his case, and not the privilege of his witnesses as such.' Furthermore it was held in Parry-Jones v. Law Society,[14] that there is a distinction between privilege and a duty not to disclose information derived from a confidential relationship, such duty being based in contract or tort. Although doctors (as other professionals) may be sued for damages for breach of such a duty of confidence, the idea of privilege is a different one and has relevance only when concern is with judicial or quasi-judicial proceedings.

The legal rules concerning privilege clearly do not afford any support for the doctor's perspective on confidentiality. Indeed the emphasis is quite clearly on the right to confidentiality or privilege as one enjoyed by the patient, if by anyone, rather than by the doctor. But any right which can be said to exist on this basis is limited in scope as it is concerned solely with the business of litigation. As such, any right to testimonial privilege is simply an extension of the traditional rights given by the law to litigants to make ready their own case, including the right not to make incriminating statements. One possible means of justifying these rights is by way of the idea of privacy, that it is not for individuals to divulge certain information but for others to prove it. But it is certainly clear that whatever the basis of the rules of privilege, it is not a question of the autonomy of the medical profession. However it is equally the case that where the law does confer the privilege its true basis is not confidentiality as such but rather the value placed by the law on litigation.[15]

2. Access to medical records.

A different approach to the principle of confidentiality can be discerned, however, when we consider the problem of access to medical records. If it were the case that there was a general right of access to data concerning individuals then such a right would be part of a right to privacy. However in the British legal system no such general right exists, although specific rights of access exist in some circumstances.[16]

The question of patients' access to medical records was considered by the Lindop Committee on Data Protection.[17] The Committee noted that medical records often contained information which was written in technical jargon such as to be comprehensible to other medical practitioners but not to the patients themselves. Furthermore, they contained clinical information about the patient's treatment and care, access to which might not always be in the patient's best interests. The Committee noted that the medical profession itself took the view that medical diagnosis and prognosis should remain confidential and hence were to be disclosed to the patient only at the doctor's discretion. Accordingly the Committee refused to make any recommendation that patients should have a right of access to their own medical records and were content with the view that data in these records were best left to the medical profession to deal with as far as disclosure was concerned.

However, one area where there has been some movement towards giving the patient access to medical records concerns the legal stage of discovery, that is seeking to obtain documents from parties not involved in a legal dispute or from the other party to a legal proceeding in order to prepare or strengthen litigation. In the

Anglo-Welsh legal system the courts had only restricted powers to order such documents to be produced but this situation was improved by the Administration of Justice Act 1970 sections 31 and 32. These sections empower the court to order production of documents in the hands of a party likely to be sued in a personal injuries case, even if the action has not yet been raised, and also to order the recovery of documents in the hands of third parties once an action has been started. However in a number of cases[18] the Court of Appeal in England sought to limit the range of application of these sections by laying down the policy that at least in the first place documents ordered to be produced by virtue of these sections should be made available not to the plaintiff himself or his legal advisors, but solely to the medical experts preparing reports on the plaintiff's behalf. In Davidson v. Lloyd Aircraft Services Ltd.[19] Lord Denning M.R. gave a number of particular reasons why this policy should be adopted:

> First, medical notes and records are very difficult for laymen to understand. They may easily misinterpret them. Second, the notes and records may include the medical men's fears of worse things to come which may disturb the patient greatly if they were known to him — such as giving him six months to live: or saying the doctor suspects a malignant cancer. Third, the records and notes may contain statements made by the patient himself or by relatives which may be embarrassing and distressing if made known.

To these he added the more general point:

> These notes and records are confidential documents. The medical man should be able to make them with the utmost frankness and without the fear they may be disclosed beyond the profession. They should not be disclosed to other persons except when the interests of justice so require. (Emphasis added)

However, the House of Lords in the case of McIvor v. Southern Health Board[20] overruled these cases and the approach adopted in them. The House accepted that once the judge had decided to exercise his power to order production of the documents he must conform to the requirement of the statute which talks of production to the applicant (the plaintiff), and in the ordinary course of litigation this would be carried out by production to his solicitor. The House also stated that there was a good justification for following this procedure, namely that it would advance the purpose of the statute by leading to settlement of actions on terms that were fair to both sides by the earliest possible disclosure of documents. The House also rejected the arguments advanced in Davidson by noting that medical advisors could assist the plaintiff and his lawyers in interpreting medical reports and that irrelevant or immaterial information could be covered up when the documents were produced or steps taken by the legal advisors to prevent such information becoming known to the plaintiff himself. Lord Diplock also added the point that:

> documents disclosed on discovery unlike evidence given in court at the trial are confidential in the sense that they may not be used for any other purpose than that of the action in which they are disclosed.[21]

It is worth noting that the Scottish courts have on the whole tended to adopt an approach similar to that of the House of Lords in McIvor. Scottish courts have for long had an inherent power to order the recovery of documents in connection with litigation and these powers were strengthened by section 1 of the Administration of Justice (Scotland) Act 1972 which empowers a court to order the production of documents or other property relevant to existing civil proceedings or to civil proceedings likely to be brought. The Scottish courts have taken the view that the whole point of these powers is to assist in the process of dispute-resolution, and accordingly if documents are thought to be relevant to actual or possible litigation they should be made available to the parties and their legal advisors. Thus in Baxter v. Lothian Health Board,[22] Lord Dunpark said:

> If it is thought to be in the interests of justice for a pursuer to recover hospital records relating to him or her, that fact must overrule the natural desire of hospitals and doctors to restrict their circulation. If effect were given to the views expressed by Lord Denning M.R. in Davidson v. Lloyd Aircraft Services Ltd....counsel for pursuers would be deprived of the opportunity, which seems to me to be essential to place them in a proper position to advise their clients, of examining the medical records with a view to ensuring that all pertinent questions are put to, and answered by, the medical men whose opinion is sought.

In contrast to the law on testimonial privilege, the rules on access to medical records adopt the doctor's rather than the patient's perspective on confidentiality. It should be apparent that this is the case, for the whole issue would scarcely arise if it were the patient's perspective which was taken, as confidentiality in this case is simply an aspect of his own rights in the doctor-patient relationship. It is worth pointing out that we need to make a distinction in this context between the medical records as mere physical objects (which will generally belong to the doctor making them or in most cases in the U.K. to the National Health Service) and the information contained in them, which the law treats as property of a separate sort. The issue is, of course, to whom does the property right in the information (rather than the documents) belong. If the perspective adopted is that of the patient, then the right is his for the information is an aspect of his right of privacy. Contrariwise if we take the doctor's perspective the answer is that the doctor retains his right to the information as resulting from the process of professional decision-making from which it originated. At times the law does appear to adopt the patient's perspective on confidentiality in justifying rules on discovery or recovery of documents. For example, in the Scottish case of Lunan v. Forresthill and Associated Hospitals,[23] Lord Stott said:

> ...the argument appeared to turn on confidentiality. The relationship between doctor and patient is, of course, confidential but where the patient has waived confidentiality, as the pursuer does here, not much, in my opinion, is left of the confidentiality point. It is true that, as Lord Guthrie pointed out in Boyle v. Glasgow Royal Infirmary 1969 S.C. 72 the records are not the property of the patient but are documents kept by the defenders for their own purposes. But these are the very circumstances that make it necessary for a diligence to be obtained and if they were to be treated as a bar to recovery of documents, few documents could ever be recovered.

However the approach generally followed by the law is that information derived from the doctor-patient relationship is confidential in the sense that it is essentially a medical matter, which belongs to the medical men, and the law will intervene against the wishes of doctors only for good reason. It was noted earlier that the law tends to place a high value on litigation as a means of resolving disputes, and so it should come as no surprise that enabling litigation to be brought is for the law a good reason for interfering with the medical-based confidentiality of medical records for the purpose of discovery. It should be stressed that this view is shared by both the earlier approach adopted by the English Court of Appeal, who attempted to restrict access of records to other medical men, on the one hand and on the other hand, the approach of the House of Lords and the Scottish courts, in which records are made available to the litigants and their legal advisors. Both approaches take as the overriding aim that of facilitating litigation and neither gives to the patient any direct right to the information itself apart from that which is necessary to achieve this goal.

By way of conclusion it should be noted that there are several issues of topicality which would not arise if it were the patient's rather than the doctor's perspective on confidentiality which were adopted.

1. Range of confidentiality. One such problem concerns the range of people who are covered by the principle of confidentiality. In some instances difficulties arise because it is not the usual doctor-patient relationship which is involved, for example the case of the occupational physician who acts on behalf of an employer as doctor to employees. There is at least on the face of it a possible conflict of duties owed by the occupational physician to the employer and to the patients. But as Bell explains[24] the occupational physician has a statutory duty in many situations to make certain information available to the employer, for instance in respect of an employee's fitness for work or his apparent over-exposure to harmful substances. In addition to this, there are the other recognised exceptions to the principle of confidentiality already noted, such as the doctor's general duty owed to society to protect others. Bell does recognise that in some cases it may not be possible to make known information unless the employee-patient consents, but it is thought that in practice consent is assumed by the presentation of the employee as a patient of the occupational physician. Whether such consent can be said to be genuine or informed consent is, of course, a different matter altogether.

Another and more significant point about the range of the principle of confidentiality is the development of the idea of extended confidentiality.[25]   This is the idea that confidentiality is not breached when information is passed from one medical practitioner to another.   Something like this notion was recognised by Lord Denning in Davidson but it should be remembered that those covered by the category of medical practitioner are many and include health care staff, secretaries, administrators and social workers. Despite this range, however, such an idea of extended confidentiality is not concerned with providing information to the patient himself but rather with maintaining knowledge within the confines of the medical professions.

2. Truth-telling in medicine.   Another area which impinges upon the principle of confidentiality but which clearly adopts the doctor's rather than the patient's perspective is the general problem of truth-telling in medicine.   Again the point is that if confidentiality can be viewed in terms of the rights of the patient, it would include the right to be told the truth concerning his condition and treatment.   However several studies show that at least in certain contexts (such as dealing with patients with cancer or schizophrenia) policies of non-disclosure or withholding the truth from patients are adopted by medical practitioners.   A distinction is sometimes drawn[26] between telling lies and not telling the truth, the argument being that while the former is always impermissible the latter may be allowed in certain circumstances.   However as Oken's study of attitudes of doctors on what to tell cancer patients shows, some doctors do admit to resorting to falsifications while the use of possibly misleading euphemisms is common.[27]   Oken notes that the general tendency is to withhold information, despite the fact that the majority of doctors themselves would prefer to be told if they were the patient.   Moreover there is little by way of justification for these practices, the most common one advanced being the broadly paternalist idea that to use them is for the patient's own good or at least prevents further harm.   However Oken himself points out that there is nothing by way of empirical evidence to suggest that telling patients that they have cancer will have deleterious consequences, such as depression or suicide.   Buchanan[28] makes the further point that what is really at issue here is whether giving the patient the information will do greater or less harm than withholding it and that

decisions on this question involve greater psychiatric expertise than that possessed by most doctors, and ultimately will depend upon moral considerations about how the patient values his own life, a matter best left for the patient's own decision.

Conclusion

In this chapter we have explored the idea of confidentiality in medical practice. Although confidentiality is important for medicine in that it allows for ease of communication with doctors, its crucial role is as a moral principle relating to the relationship between doctor and patient. However, it was argued that two different points of view about confidentiality can be adopted, each of which has different values at its core. On the one hand, there is the patient's perspective, which stresses the right of privacy of the patient within the medical relationship. On the other hand, the doctor's perspective on confidentiality places emphasis on the professional autonomy of the doctor. The point about this difference in perspective is that both points of view are reflected in current discussion about the nature of confidentiality in medicine, discussion which in turn reflects a wider debate on the nature of medicine itself. As far as the law is concerned, it is not easy to say that one perspective alone predominates. The law is itself concerned with developing rules to make litigation as effective as possible as a means of resolving disputes, and it is this value which is overriding in this respect. But in a legal system like the British, which does not explicitly recognise a right to privacy, in so far as any one perspective on confidentiality is adopted, it is that of the doctor rather than the patient which predominates. Yet it is important to get right the values which do, and ought to, underlie the principle of confidentiality, for to do so will bring out much of interest about the doctor-patient relationship. Although confidentiality is only one aspect of that relationship, it does have implications for more general ideas about the role of medicine, and it is to some of these we now turn.

1. Thompson, I.E., 'The Nature of Confidentiality' (1979) 5 J. Medical Ethics 57.

2. The Handbook of Medical Ethics, British Medical Association, London 1981, paras. 1.5 - 1.7. See also, paras. 1.3, 1.12 - 1.14, 3.1 - 3.4., 10.2.

3. For further discussion on testimonial privilege, see infra, pp. 178-181.

4. Samuels, A., 'The Duty of the Doctor to Respect the Confidence of the Patient' (1980) 20 Med. Sci & Law, 58, at p. 59.

5. [1974] 1 Q.B. 767.

6. per Boreham J. at p. 774.

7. Thompson, loc.cit., at p. 58.

8. This difference in the nature of the doctor-patient relationship is examined further in chapter 10, infra.

9. (1964) 2 The Lancet 145.

10. [1963] 2 Q.B. 477, at pp. 489-490.

11. [1974] 1 Q.B. 767, at p. 775.

12. [1955] 2 Q.B. 195.

13. ibid. at pp. 202-3.

14. [1969] 1 Ch. 1.

15. c.f. McPhail, I.D., Research Paper on the Law of Evidence of Scotland, Scottish Law Commission, April 1979, para. 18-20.

16. For example, the Consumer Credit Act 1974 sections 158-9, give a person the right to obtain from a credit reference agency information relating to himself and also to require such agencies to correct erroneous information on their files.

17. Cmnd. 7341/1978, especially chapters 7 and 24.

18. See for example, Davidson v. Lloyd Aircraft Services Ltd. [1974] 1 W.L.R. 1042; Deistung v. S.W. Metropolitan Health Board [1975] 1 W.L.R. 213.

19. [1974] 1 W.L.R. 1042, at p. 1046.

20. [1978] 1 W.L.R. 757.

21. ibid., at p. 767.

22. 1976 S.L.T. (Notes) 37, at p. 38. See the similar view expressed by Lord Grieve in McGown v. Erskine & ors. 1978 S.L.T. (Notes) 4.

23. 1975 S.L.T. (Notes) 40, at p. 40.

24. Bell, J.D., 'The Occupational Physician and the Law', in McLean, S.A.M., (ed) Legal Issues in Medicine, Aldershot, Gower Publishing Co., 1981, at pp. 19-22.

25. Mason, J.K., Forensic Medicine for Lawyers, Bristol, John Wright & Sons, 1978, at p. 384; Dworkin, G., 'Access to Medical Records - Discovery, Confidentiality and Privacy' (1979) 42 Modern Law Review 88, at p. 90; Phelby, D.P.H., 'Changing practice on confidentiality: a cause for concern' (1982) 8 J. Medical Ethics 12.

26. Salzman, L., 'Truth, Honesty and the Therapeutic Process' (1973) 130 American Journal of Psychiatry 1280, at p. 1281.

27. Oken, D., 'What to Tell Cancer Patients: A Study of Medical Attitudes' (1961) 175 Journal of the American Medical Association 1120.

28. Buchanan, A., 'Medical Paternalism' (1978) 7 Philosophy and Public Affairs 370, at p. 377.

10 Decision-making in Medicine

It might be thought that the subject of decision-making in medicine lacks the obvious relevance to the fields of morals and law which is a feature of the other topics examined in this book. However it is in many ways appropriate to conclude a book concerned with the interaction of medicine, morals and the law with consideration of medical decision-making, for not only does decision-making involve many problems of responsibility, both legal and moral, but it also raises many questions about the nature of medicine itself and the related concepts of health, illness and disease. In general terms, the conclusion of the argument (and it is one that acts as an appropriate conclusion of the book itself) is that not all decisions taken by medical practitioners are genuinely 'medical' in nature, and this is so even if we limit our attention to those decisions clearly and unarguably within the scope of medical practice. Indeed there are those who argue that so long as we refuse to examine critically current modes of medical decision-making, we run the risk not only of confusion of thought but also of danger both to health and to social and political values such as personal autonomy.

The common-sense idea of a medical decision is relatively clear-cut and virtually all of us have experienced, even if not actually made, such a decision. The most typical example occurs in the everyday experience of a visit by a patient to his or her GP. Generally speaking we visit a GP because we expect him or her to be able to do something for us, such as to identify or diagnose a pain which we experience and to decide upon the most appropriate way of dealing with the problem (eg the issuing of a prescription of a pain-killing drug with instructions as to the proper dose). Although this example is no doubt a very common experience, we should not think it to be insignificant in terms of illustrating the essential features of much medical practice and as setting out the background against which most medical decisions are made.

Indeed it is possible to state a number of assumptions which are thought to underlie our everyday understanding of medical practice. Although there is no definitive list of such assumptions, the most important for our purposes are as follows.

1.   Doctors are experts in medicine, an expertise derived from a technical training (usually very expensive to provide) and from wide-ranging practical experience.

2.   Medicine, a specialist field of knowledge, is a science (i.e. a discipline with a coherent and systematic body of tested learning) that can be applied by those expert in it, and one whose mastery depends upon knowledge of its specialised techniques, ideas and language (often incomprehensible to the non-expert).

3.   The social practice known as medicine is as a matter of fact a successful one, in that it is effective in what it seeks to do.

4.   The aim of medicine is to promote health, most typically by seeking to put right illness or disease which attacks health. The crucial point about this assumption of modern medical practice is that the general concepts of health and illness (and disease) are treated as unproblematic. The question of the existence or indications of particular illnesses is a question within medical science, but the general ideas are relatively unexplored.

5.   An extension of this last-stated assumption is that the role of medicine is essentially interventionist, that is its function is to promote a cure once illness or disease has manifested itself. In particular health is seen as the absence of any dysfunction of the parts of the body (including the mind), and medicine is the activity of correcting such dysfunctions.

All of these assumptions about medicine and medical practice may at first glance appear obvious but each of them is questionable and is being questioned. In this concluding chapter, specific attention is paid to the last three of these assumptions which together illustrate the weaknesses of the model of medicine commonly used in consideration of medical decision-making.

How 'medical' are decisions in medicine?

As a starting-point to developing the general argument, let us consider a number of instances where it can be argued there are medical decisions in areas which go beyond the boundaries of what is generally considered to be medicine. We examined above[1] some of the workings of the law relating to abortion in Great Britain. It will be remembered that the general position at law is that abortion is forbidden unless the case falls within one of a number of exceptions, the most important of which are those specified in the Abortion Act 1967. The Act permits abortion in certain specified circumstances where two medical practitioners are of the opinion that to continue rather than to terminate a pregnancy would cause serious risk to the mother's life or health, or to the life or health of her family. When considering whether the case falls within the provisions of the Act the doctors may take account of the mother's environment (either her actual or reasonably foreeable environment).

Several points about the workings of the Act have already been noted. One is that the Act provides no rights to the foetus (such as the right to be born), nor to the father (such as the right to be consulted on the termination of the pregnancy). Furthermore it provides no rights to the mother, even if, objectively considered, her case falls within the terms of the Act since she cannot require that an abortion be performed on her. The crucial role is that of the two medical practitioners who have the power to decide, within the law, whether an abortion should be carried out. Further, the courts have accepted that it is not for them to supervise in detail how doctors operate the Act, responsibility for which lies with the medical profession.

At this point we must pause and ask whether this state of affairs is at all defensible. The Act does use a medical model, in that it requires certain medical questions (e.g. the risk to the mother's life from continuation of the pregnancy) to be answered, but the further decision as to whether or not to perform an abortion once

192

these questions have been resolved is not itself medical. Rather it raises moral questions about the propriety of ending foetal life, questions which feature in the general debate about the legalisation of abortion. Now it does not necessarily follow that the medical profession come to the 'wrong' conclusions in deciding these matters. The point is rather that the resolution of such questions hardly calls for medical expertise. Nor is it simply matters of moral principle which are involved, for issues of social welfare are also at stake in so far as the Act explicitly allows for the mother's environment to be taken into account when deciding in certain cases upon the risk involved in the continuation of the pregnancy. This is why the actual workings of the Act lead to some objectionable practices, the foremost of which is the wide regional variations in resort to the Abortion Act.[2] If society, acting through the law, decides that abortion is permissible under certain circumstances, it is to say the least odd that some women cannot avail themselves of facilities with the same ease as other women merely because of the region in which they happen to live.[3] Yet this is the predictable result of entrusting what are essentially moral and social decisions to a group of people whose expertise lies in other fields.

Another example of the range of considerations involved in medical decision-making, and one which shows clearly how moral and social issues are disguised by labelling them as medical in nature, is that of euthanasia. It was argued in chapter 3 above that although the formal legal position is that euthanasia is equivalent to murder, the actual administration of the criminal law paints a very different picture.[4] In particular the acceptance by certain sides of the medical profession of passive as opposed to active euthanasia (a distinction which is in itself highly questionable) is also apparently accepted by the law, in that cases where death has resulted from a failure to act by a doctor will rarely lead to conviction of a criminal offence or even to prosecution. Indeed it may well be that medical practice adopts the position it does partly because of what is perceived to be legal practice on this matter. It was further noted earlier that leaving the issues of euthanasia and terminating treatment in the hands of the medical profession has been advocated openly as a proper way of resolving the difficult issues involved.

However, this whole approach should be carefully examined. It is far from obvious that decisions about euthanasia can be resolved by applying purely medical considerations; on the contrary the difficulties presented by the issue are, if they are anything, social and moral in nature. It may indeed be that the distressing nature of many instances of mercy-killing has the result that most of us do not want to face up to these issues. But if this is the case, then our practice should be recognised for what it is, namely a failure to take seriously an important moral problem. It might appear to be easier to leave these issues in the hands of the medical profession but if we wish the true nature of euthanasia to be identified and resolved, then we must not disguise the issues as involving technical questions of medicine. It is not at all apparent what parts of the euthanasia debate can best be taken as involving technical medical issues or what special expertise the medical profession can claim in resolving the dispute.

As a final example of a 'medical' decision, we can consider the area of allocation of scarce medical resources.[5] The problems involved in this area are illustrated by the sort of case where we have a number of patients in excess of a particular piece of medical equipment or skill, with the result that not all can be treated. Such cases often involve scarce resources such as organs suitable for purposes of transplantation, or advanced technology such as haemodialysis used to treat kidney disorders. We should note that the effect of scarcity of such resources is that we are quite literally deciding upon the life and death of each patient involved. Thus if there are ten patients with chronic kidney failure and there is only one dialysis machine, the decision to give the treatment to one patient means certain death for the other nine. How then are such decisions made and how ought they to be arrived at?

One possible solution is to say that although at present certain medical facilities, such as expensive technology, are scarce in the sense that there is not enough for everyone who needs it, ideally there ought to be enough and that ideal is one which we should seek to attain. In other words, we should spend more on such resources and (to continue our example) we should have ten rather than one dialysis machine. However this solution does not solve the immediate problem where there is a situation of actual scarcity. Moreover, it is of dubious value as a general approach to allocating medical resources, for it presupposes that the cost of technology is better spent than some alternative allocation within the health service. But it may well be that the cost of advanced technology in medicine is way out of proportion to its relative 'success' or 'efficiency', and that money would be better spent in some other way.[6] So although this approach does appear to solve the problem of scarcity at one level, it does so only by ignoring other dimensions of the question, a point which will be mentioned further once we examine the general ideas of health and medicine.

An idea that is sometimes advanced is that a distinction can be drawn between general issues of allocation of social resources to health and medicine (e.g. how much public finance to invest in the health service rather than, for example, defence) and specific issues concerning the deployment of existing medical resources. It is generally thought that the first sort of decision falls to be determined in accordance with the normal means of deciding political matters (and so the issues involved are not treated as medical ones), whereas the second sort are purely medical, for resolution solely by the medical profession itself. However, this view depends for its plausibility upon a particular conception of health and medicine (discussed later in this chapter) which clearly marks off medicine from social and moral considerations. Moreover, even in the case of decisions about the allocation of existing medical resources, the view that these are purely medical matters is questionable.

What then is the basis for decisions about the allocation of scarce medical resources? One point which should be stressed at this stage is that there are really two separate (though related) issues here. One is that of the most appropriate criteria for making decisions of this nature. But a second is equally important: who is to decide the matter? Indeed, some writers have argued that it is not enough to arrive at the correct conclusions to these problems but we must also devise procedures which themselves display the fairness of the manner in which decisions are made.[7]

Take first of all some of the criteria suggested as the basis for deciding who is to receive scarce medical resources. The criteria we shall discuss should not be taken as exhaustive of possible solutions but they do illustrate the factors relevant to discussions of the problem. Furthermore, although some comment will

195

be made about each criterion, it should be borne in mind that our concern is more with the sort of consideration involved in each criterion than with assessing its correctness as an answer, or partial answer, to the original problem.

1.   One criterion often mentioned especially by medical practitioners is that of likelihood of success. In other words we must give resources to those who are likely to respond to the treatment. Thus, for example, patients requiring dialysis treatment who do not also have cardiovascular conditions are to be preferred to those who do. But two points should be noted about this suggestion. One is that it does not guarantee solving the problem in every case, for although we can eliminate some patients as less suitable for receiving specific treatment (e.g. organ transplantation, use of a dialysis machine) than others, it is likely that we would still have to choose between patients all of equal standing in terms of this factor. It might be thought that the likelihood of success should then be treated as a necessary but not a sufficient part of the solution to the problem. But we should note a second general point. This is that it is by no means as clear-cut as it may appear what is meant by 'success' of medical treatment. We can only say that something is (or is not) successful if we know what it is seeking to achieve. But what exactly is the aim of treating (say) patients with kidney failure? It may appear intuitively plausible to say that if we can predict that dialysis treatment would let patient A live for ten years and patient B for only five, then we should select A over B if only one of them can receive the treatment, but this takes no account of the quality of life involved. We must therefore make more explicit why such a selection accords with the nature of 'successful' treatment, and when we do this we shall find that we are confronted with non-medical questions about what constitutes a worthwhile life.

2.   Another criterion is that of the potential future contribution of the patient. The basic idea here is to assess the return to society which use of the resource would give in respect of each potential patient. The point could be stated negatively by seeking to exclude those whose non-treatment would present the least social cost or burden. Presumably this would mean that, all other things being

equal, we would select for treatment a banker rather than a tramp, for we live in a society in which as a matter of fact the lives of bankers are valued more highly than the lives of tramps. But this criterion, quite apart from any objection there may be in principle to the idea of measuring the value of different lives, also presents practical problems about the commensurability of different lives. Is a lawyer of more social value than a doctor? Or a young politician more important than an elderly poet? Clearly, such decisions cannot be properly called medical.

3. A third criterion requires us to look to the past services rendered by the patient and select patients according to their prior social contribution. The underlying idea here is to select on the basis of merit or desert. This has a ring of justice to it, but in addition to problems of commensurability similar to those involved in the future contribution factor, this factor taken by itself could lead to counter-intuitive results (e.g. it could mean that the elderly would almost always be preferred to the young). In any case, the decisions involved are hardly medical in nature.

4. Another criterion, though it is one rarely explicitly mentioned in discussion of this problem and is clearly non-medical, is that of the market. Treatment would be available to those who can pay for it and where there is scarcity of resources treatment would go to the highest bidder. If this solution strikes us as odd (and it certainly seems odd to many people) we should note that we do use the market to allocate other scarce resources and we should reflect on what it is about health and medicine which makes it inappropriate to allocate them by means of the market.

5. A final criterion is that of random selection. This might be necessary either because having applied all other proper criteria we still are in a position of scarcity or because we are using different criteria which cannot be traded off against each other. The advantage of such a criterion may well be that it does relieve the decision-makers of what might be thought to be their responsibility in situations where there is no obviously correct solution (or even means of arriving at one).

These criteria are illustrative of those suggested as appropriate for decisions about use of medical resources. Now what should strike us as obvious about them is that they are not medical in nature. Certainly the primary decision to adopt one (or more) as the proper standard cannot be medical in nature. But even the application of any particular criterion is hardly something that calls primarily for medical expertise. The nearest we get to this is criterion (1), that is the likelihood of success, but we have already noted that this standard presupposes that we know what is meant by 'successful' medical treatment. The other factors, such as services rendered or the future social contribution of the patient can hardly be thought ones which doctors are particularly qualified to be able to assess.

This point is worth making for the following reason. This discussion should not be thought of merely as an academic exercise in moral philosophy or decision-making, for situations of scarcity of resources are ones which confront health services in most countries at present. Indeed it is likely that the more we continue to concentrate on expensive high technology medical resources, the more such scarcity will increase. It should be something of a surprise therefore to discover that in the United Kingdom at least, decisions about medical resources are treated as ones which doctors must make. In the United States there have been some moves to institute compulsory consultation with non-medical opinion in dealing with these matters but it is thought that the effect of these measures has been negligible. Yet to say the least it is very odd that such decisions are treated as medical ones calling for medical expertise, for many if not indeed all of the factors put forward as being of relevance to such issues are not medical in nature (at least not in the sense of medicine adopted so far).

Yet consider a symposium on selection of patients for haemodialysis given by a hospital physician, a consultant in clinical renal physiology, a surgeon professor of urology, and a general practitioner.[8] Although the point that social aspects were of relevance to the issue was noted in the discussion, none of the symposiasts was willing to accept that there was any role for lay persons in making such decisions. This conclusion was arrived at by a variety of ways. First it was said that the doctor knows the

198

medical aspect of the patient, thus ignoring the point that more than
the medical factors are involved. Secondly it was said that doctors
are experts in making such decisions, but this is simply begging the
question whether they ought to be the only ones with the opportunity
to decide on such matters. Finally it was argued that the burden of
responsibility should not be on lay people, but again if the issues
are wider than the narrowly medical, then the responsibility is
already on everyone, and it is questionable whether this is properly
discharged by disguising the issues as medical and leaving them for
the medical profession to resolve. It should also be noted that one
of the symposiasts thought that the best contribution which laymen
could make was to try to raise funds to provide more dialysis
machines! All of this takes no account of the fact that doctors are
not trained as 'experts' in matters of social policy or moral
philosophy, and are liable to concentrate on 'medical' aspects of such
decisions to the exclusion of those wider issues in which they have no
obvious monopoly of wisdom.

The role of medicine.

A possible objection to the argument presented so far is that the
examples discussed, abortion, euthanasia, and allocation of scarce
medical resources, are somehow not typical of medicine or do not
illustrate the main issues of concern to medical decision-making.
Thus it could be argued that although some matters decided by doctors
go beyond the strict limits of medicine, these instances are truly
peripheral and should not be confused with the central matters of
medicine. Indeed a rejoinder such as this can be backed up with an
appeal to the very powerful point that as a matter of fact medicine is
a successful activity, and that the interventionist model of modern
medicine, which takes medical decisions as technical ones for medical
experts, can (to say the least) be justified by its actual
contribution to health.

But such a claim calls for supporting evidence. Surprisingly
perhaps, a number of writers have claimed that modern medicine has not
contributed to health, and indeed some also claim that it is
positively dangerous not just to our health but also to political

freedom. These arguments require some consideration here and have importance for the present discussion, for they suggest not only that medicine may not be as 'successful' as it might be considered to be but also that our very ideas of health and medicine may disguise issues of responsibility and lead us to fail to appreciate what is involved in medical decision-making.

One major contribution to this debate has been the work of McKeown.[9]   McKeown's main concern is with analysing and explaining the improvement in health in England and Wales during the course of the nineteenth century and the role of medicine in this development. In essence his claim is that the nineteenth century did witness improvements in health as indicated by the decline in mortality rates, and also the rise of an organised medical profession using an interventionist approach to medicine.   But McKeown argues that it is wrong to attribute a causal link between these two factors.   Rather the improvement in health was caused by a variety of factors, the most important of which can be called environmental, namely improvement in nutrition and in hygiene.   Another factor of significance was the change in reproductive practices which led to a decline in the birth-rate, as this meant that such improvements in health as did follow from other means were not threatened by rising numbers.   Last, and least in terms of effectiveness behind these environmental and behavioural factors, are therapeutic ones.   McKeown argues that immunisation and therapy had little effect on national mortality trends until 1935 (with the exception of vaccination against smallpox) and even since then have not been the most important factor.[10]

Although much of McKeown's work is concerned with assessing the claims to success by medicine in its historical context, his analysis also applies to the present time.   For him, a crucial distinction is that between abnormalities determined irreversibly at fertilisation and those which are manifested only in an appropriate environment. McKeown suggests that instances of the first type are relatively rare and that:

> the large majority of diseases and disabilities are neither simply inherited nor otherwise determined irreversibly at fertilization; they are usually described as multifactorial, by which is meant that they are caused by interaction between multiple environmental and genetic influences.[11]

McKeown also points out that those diseases and disabilities in which
the environmental influences are post-natal (and he argues that these
include nearly all the common diseases and disabilities, including
cancer) could in principle be prevented by appropriate environmental
modification (though he accepts that some of these modifications
involve public or private decisions which may be difficult to
accept).[12]

In a society like ours the relevant environmental conditions
which have an influence on ill-health are those of bad diet (which in
the economically developed countries means eating too much and of the
wrong food, in contrast to the developing countries where
undernourishment is the main problem at times confounded with the
availability of Western style mass-produced food), lack of exercise,
smoking and accidents (mainly those at home, at work and on the road).

There are many implications which McKeown's work (and that of
others such as Dubos[13]) have for our present concern but two at
least should be expressly stated now. One is that the
interventionist model of medicine is doomed to failure in that it
allots a role to medicine which is simply too late in making its
contribution to the promotion of health. Good health would be better
promoted by seeking to discourage or prevent the environment in which
illness is manifested. For example, although some people may be
genetically prone to diabetes a more effective contribution to dealing
with diabetes would be to ensure that such people lived in a 'healthy
environment' (such as one where food was not highly processed or where
refined sugar was not consumed) so that the disease was not triggered
off; this rather than waiting for the disease to appear and then seek
to control (but note, not cure) it by treatment with insulin. A
second point follows on from this one, namely that decisions about
health and illness cannot avoid matters which go beyond technical
questions of bodily functions and dysfunctions. Given that health is
partly a matter of such diverse social and moral issues as the sort of
food which is permitted to be made and sold, the sort and limitations
imposed on sexual behaviour and reproduction, the level of
unemployment and so on[14], medicine cannot be separated from these
wider issues. This reinforces the points made when discussing the
examples of abortion, euthanasia and allocation of medical
resources. One conclusion which might be drawn from that discussion

is that certain decisions made by medical practitioners involve considerations beyond the purely technically medical and accordingly we should no longer treat them as really medical. However another way of looking at the situation goes in the opposite direction: this is that such issues truly _are_ medical in nature but given the view of health and medicine which they adopt, decisions affecting them cannot be the sole prerogative of medical practitioners.

Conclusion: the concepts of health and medicine.

This argument can be presented by reference to the lively and continuing debate about the very ideas of health and medicine. We have already seen that one of the implications of McKeown's work is that the idea of ill-health cannot be separated from the general environment in which ill-health is manifested. Other writers have stated this same point in a more positive manner by arguing that the determination of what counts as health is not a 'technical' matter at all, but is instead a value-judgment which uses a range of social and moral values.[15] Similarly if medicine is at all thought to be concerned with the promotion of health (or at least the prevention or cure of ill-health), then it must be concerned with the general issues of how society is and ought to be structured.

But why then should modern medicine have given itself the technical interventionist role it has adopted? One reason is that there are vested interests in the present state of affairs. It is possible to identify different levels of such vested interests. One is that of the medical profession itself, for its control (given the interventionist model) of the use of the label 'illness' is a source of power. It has for some time now been argued that the very idea of mental illness is illusory, but (it is argued) its continued use permits doctors to control people who deviate in some way from a social norm, usually in ways which are much harsher than the manner in which other social deviants (such as criminals) are treated. But it has also been argued that the monopoly which the medical profession enjoys as to the use of the labels 'physical health' and 'physical ill-health' likewise gives them considerable political power.

Other vested interests in the status quo are those who benefit from those current environmental conditions which play a role in causing ill-health. These include manufacturers of alcohol, tobacco and motor-vehicles, all groups with much political power in society and who would be threatened by attempts to attack ill-health by changing those environmental factors or habits from which they benefit. Another such group is that of pharmaceutical manufacturers. It is by now a familiar story of the huge profits which drug manufacturers make and the control which they have over the medical professions to ensure the continued use of their products. Again the point has been made emphatically that the majority of modern drugs cannot be thought to be 'successful' in curing illness or disease already manifested. On the contrary this is one of the examples which Illich uses in his discussion of 'clinical iatrogenesis', that is the actual physical damage which is caused to people by the interventionist mode of medicine. But a fundamental point about the place of the pharmaceutical industry in modern medicine is that it would cease to exist if the assumptions of modern medicine were abandoned. As long as medicine confines its role to that of putting right technical dysfunctions of the body as a machine, there will be scope for drugs and technology to assist them in so doing. As Illich writes, 'To blame the drug industry for prescribed-drug addiction is therefore as irrelevant as blaming the Mafia for the use of illicit drugs'[16]

However it is worth noting at this point that, although some of the so-called anti-medicine literature may state otherwise, there is nothing inherently wrong about the use of drugs and technology to promote health and to prevent illness. Nor is it true to say that all pharmaceutical and technological devices currently used in modern medicine are either unsuccessful (but harmless) or positively a form of iatrogenesis.[17] The point is rather that there is something wrong with our concepts of medicine and health which allot such a direct and central part to curing illness by these means, often at great expense and with questionable benefits. As a corollary of this general point it must not be thought that there are no technical issues within the field of medicine which call for resolution by experts. To believe this would be as mistaken as to believe that such matters were the sole business of medicine.

Furthermore, it should not be thought that the nature of modern medicine is peculiarly the consequence of powerful interests (though these interests should not be underestimated). For in many ways, it suits us as a society to accept a situation whereby certain matters are given a technical tag as 'medical' and can then be entrusted to a body of experts for their resolution. Several writers have observed a parallel between the role played by the doctor in modern society and the role of the priest or religious man in earlier times.[18] There is clearly a powerful social need for a broad form of knowledge which helps to explain the world and helps us to cope with difficult and distressing situations. But this is a trend which is fraught with dangers. Illich discusses these dangers in terms of structural iatrogenesis, that is the destruction of a person's political and moral autonomy by a social system in which illness is thought of as a matter for medical experts alone to determine. Similarly Kennedy talks of the dangers of allowing the power presently allotted to doctors without checks on this power and adds: 'It is hard to overstate how such a social arrangement may undermine the notion of individual responsibility and of course, ultimately, of individual liberty'.[19]

Despite the apparent paradox, an appropriate place to conclude this book is the introduction of the debate on medical nemesis and related controversies on the nature of medicine. What we have sought to show is that the fields of medicine, morals and the law are not simply capable of throwing interesting light on each other, but that by its very nature medicine involves the points of view of law, morals and other social disciplines. If law is too important to be left to lawyers, then medicine is too central a social institution to be entrusted solely to medical practitioners.

NOTES

1. See supra, chapter 2.

2. (Lane) Report of the Committee on the Working of the Abortion Act, Cmnd 5579/1975, Vol.1, para. 43, Figs. CIII-VII.

3. Lane Report, paras. 186 et seq. on the issue of who is to make decisions under the Act.

4. see supra, at pp. 56-7.

5. See further, Rescher, N., 'The Allocation of Exotic Medical Lifesaving Therapy' (1969) <u>79</u> <u>Ethics</u> 173; Note, 'Patient Selection for Artificial and Transplanted Organs' (1969) <u>82</u> <u>Harvard Law Review</u> 1322; Leenan, H.J.J., 'Selection of Patients' (1982) <u>8</u> <u>J. Medical Ethics</u> 33.

6. On the question of the nature of the 'success' of technology-oriented medicine, see further chapter 6, supra. In the U.K., 70% of the N.H.S. budget is spent on hospitals but this allocation has been criticised as wasteful: Doyal, L., <u>The Political Economy of Health</u>, London, Pluto Press, 1979, at pp. 195-197; Kennedy, I., <u>The Unmasking of Medicine</u>, London, George Allen & Unwin, 1981, at p. 32.

7. Rescher, loc.cit., at p. 175.

8. Symposium, 'Selection of Patients for Haemodialysis' <u>British Medical Journal</u>, 11 March 1967, pp. 622-624.

9. See especially, McKeown, <u>The Role of Medicine</u>, London, Nuffield Provincial Hospitals Trust, 1976.

10. See McKeown, op.cit., at pp. 93-4, for a summary of the argument.

11. ibid., at p. 17.

12. ibid., at pp.27-8.

13. Dubos, R., <u>The Mirage of Health</u>, London, George Allen & Unwin, 1960; <u>Man, Medicine and Environment</u>, London, Pall Mall Press, 1968.

14. A debate has arisen recently about the connection between the national economy and health. More particularly, Professor Harvey Brenner has claimed that there is a causal link between unemployment and ill health, including mortality; see Brenner, M.H., 'Mortality and the National Economy: A review and the Experience of England and Wales, 1936-1976', <u>The Lancet</u>, 15 September 1979, pp. 568-573; Graville, H.S.E., et al., 'Mortality and Unemployment: A Critique of Brenner's Time-Series Analysis', <u>The Lancet</u>, 26 September 1981, pp. 675-681; Brenner, M.H., 'Unemployment and Health', <u>The Lancet</u>, 17 October 1981, pp.874-5. This debate is summarised in an article in the <u>Times Health Supplement</u>, 30 October 1981, pp. 14-15.

15. See especially, Illich, I., <u>Limits to Medicine. Medical</u>

Nemesis: The Expropriation of Health, Harmondsworth, Penguin
Books, 1977 edition;   Kennedy, op.cit.

16.   Illich, op.cit., at pp. 81-2.

17.   See McKeown, op.cit., at p. 167.

18.   See, for example, Szasz, T., *The Theology of Medicine*, London,
O.U.P., 1979.

19.   Kennedy, op.cit., at p. 18.

Index

Giertz, G., 124.

Glover, J., 13; 14; 18; 22; 40; 58; 65; 77; 78.

Gonzales, B., 147.

Gordon, L., 147.

Gordon, G.H., 102; 130; 148.

Gravelle, H.S.E., 205.

Grieve, Lord, 188.

haemodialysis, 17; 194; 198.

haemophilia, 139.

Hart, H.L.A., 39; 40; 41; 59.

Havard, J.D.J., 77.

Hilton, B., 147.

Hippocratic Oath, 2; 104; 170; 173.

Hodson, Lord Justice, 180.

Honore, A.M., 59.

human life, boundaries of, 7-8; 21-24; 61-62; 64.

hypothermia, 17.

Illich, I., 6; 18; 101; 109; 121; 122; 123; 144; 149; 153; 154; 168; 171; 172; 203; 204; 205; 206.

incest, 135.

infants, 31; 47; 49; 63; 66; 141.

in vitro fertilisation, 7; 125.

Jehovah's witnesses, 72.

Katz, J., 123; 124.

Kennedy, I., 101; 102; 108; 123; 124; 163; 172; 204; 205; 206.

Kilbrandon, Lord, 148.

Klass, A., 123.

Kohl, M., 59.

Nicholson, R., 58.

Oken, D., 186; 189.
omissions, 15–16; 51–53; 68; 69; 71; 74.
ordinary/extraordinary treatment, see proportionate/disproportionate
    means.

paternalism, 68; 85; 86; 90; 91; 94; 135; 186.
Pearson Report, Royal Commission on Civil Liability and Compensation
    for Personal Injuries, 164.
Pellegrino, E., 81; 101; 102; 123; 124; 171; 172.
pharmaceutical industry, 105; 107–108; 203.
Phelby, D.P.H., 189.
pneumonia, 74.
Pope Pius XII, 63.
potential life, 24; 28–31; 35; 49; 65.
privacy, 22; 133; 171; 181; 187.
proportionate/disproportionate means, 53; 63–64.

quality of life, see worth-while life.
quickening, 21–22.

Rachels, J., 52; 58.
Reilly, P., 148.
religious belief, 8–9; 46; 127; 133; 135–136.
replaceability (of people), 11; 64; 65; 73.
Research Ethical Committees, 113.
Rescher, N., 205.
respect for persons, see autonomy-based ethics.
reverence for life, 2–3; 6.
rights, moral, 12; 24–28; 37–38; 46–47; 64–65; 69; 82; 83;
    86; 90–92; 97; 98; 116; 119; 122; 125; 126; 130–131;
    134–136; 138–139; 142–143; 145; 152; 177; 181; 184; 192.
    right to be born, 25; 27–28; 37; 145.